PSYCHOLOGY OF EMOTIONS, MOTIVATIONS AND ACTIONS



# FIREARMS AND SUICIDE

# IS PREVENTION POSSIBLE?

# PSYCHOLOGY OF EMOTIONS, MOTIVATIONS AND ACTIONS

Additional books and e-books in this series can be found on Nova's website under the Series tab.

PSYCHOLOGY OF EMOTIONS, MOTIVATIONS AND ACTIONS

# FIREARMS AND SUICIDE

## IS PREVENTION POSSIBLE?

DAVID LESTER
EDITOR

nova
science publishers
New York

## NOTICE TO THE READER

The Publisher has taken reasonable care in the preparation of this book, but makes no expressed or implied warranty of any kind and assumes no responsibility for any errors or omissions. No liability is assumed for incidental or consequential damages in connection with or arising out of information contained in this book. The Publisher shall not be liable for any special, consequential, or exemplary damages resulting, in whole or in part, from the readers' use of, or reliance upon, this material. Any parts of this book based on government reports are so indicated and copyright is claimed for those parts to the extent applicable to compilations of such works.

Independent verification should be sought for any data, advice or recommendations contained in this book. In addition, no responsibility is assumed by the Publisher for any injury and/or damage to persons or property arising from any methods, products, instructions, ideas or otherwise contained in this publication.

This publication is designed to provide accurate and authoritative information with regard to the subject matter covered herein. It is sold with the clear understanding that the Publisher is not engaged in rendering legal or any other professional services. If legal or any other expert assistance is required, the services of a competent person should be sought. FROM A DECLARATION OF PARTICIPANTS JOINTLY ADOPTED BY A COMMITTEE OF THE AMERICAN BAR ASSOCIATION AND A COMMITTEE OF PUBLISHERS.

Additional color graphics may be available in the e-book version of this book.

**Library of Congress Cataloging-in-Publication Data**

Names: Lester, David, 1942- editor.
Title: Firearms and suicide : is prevention possible? / editor, David Lester, Ph.D.
(Stockton University, Galloway, NJ, USA).
Description: Hauppauge, New York: Nova Science Publishers, Inc., [2018] |
Series: Psychology of emotions, motivations and actions | Includes index.
Identifiers: LCCN 2018050892 | ISBN 9781536146905 (softcover)
Subjects: LCSH: Gun control. | Firearms accidents. | Suicide--Prevention.
Classification: LCC HV7435 .F56 2018 | DDC 363.33--dc23 LC record available at https://lccn.loc.gov/2018050892

*Published by Nova Science Publishers, Inc. † New York*

# CONTENTS

# PREFACE

In 2018, after many mass murders at schools in the United States, the role of firearms in homicide has received much greater serious attention than hitherto. Proposals have been made to prevent such mass murders, ranging from arming school teachers to banning access to some types of guns and ammunition magazines.

Less attention has been focused on the role of firearms in suicidal behavior, although several suicidology organizations have issued statements, made proposals and engaged in activity, including the American Foundation for Suicide Prevention (AFSP) and the American Association of Suicidology (AAS).

It is important to note that many of the proposals for preventing mass murders using firearms have little applicability to suicide prevention. Obviously, arming teachers is irrelevant, but so is a proposal to ban the sale of semi-automatic firearms, such as the AK-47 or the AR-15. My search of the literature found only one suicide using a semi-automatic firearm, that by a soldier in Israel.

The purpose of the present book is to review the research on firearms and suicide. What do we know and what research do we need to conduct in order to better understand and, therefore, prevent firearm suicide. This has been a focus of my research for all of my career in suicidology, and so I will review my own research on this topic in Chapter 1. I will also review the research conducted by others in Chapter 2. In addition, I have asked experts from Canada (Antoon Leenaars, Robert Olson, and Karin Lavoie) and from Australia (Karolina Krysinska) to review the field from the perspective of their country. There has been some controversy over the involvement of suicide prevention organizations with firearm organizations, and so I have asked a suicidology scholar who is also a gun owner (John Gunn) to discuss how those concerned with preventing suicide might work with those in firearm organizations and those in the firearms business. Finally, I will review proposals for preventing firearm suicide.

Restricting access to firearms as a means of suicide prevention is part of a larger strategy. A great deal of research has explored the role of restricting access to lethal means for suicide, including methods for suicide such as:

1. coal gas (especially as a result of the switch from coal gas to natural gas for domestic use)
2. car exhaust
3. medications, both prescriptions and over-the-counter medications
4. pesticides
5. jumping from high places
6. trains

The research on these methods for suicide has been reviewed by Clarke and Lester (1989, 2013) and Lester (2009) and, overall, the strategy has proved to be beneficial in that suicides using those methods are reduced when access to the methods is restricted. Restricting access to the methods listed above does not run into much opposition. For example, it was not difficult to reduce the number of pills per bottle of acetaminophen (paracetamol and Tylenol) in bottles that are sold over the counter and to place them in plastic blisters.

In some cases, the changes necessary were not made to prevent suicide, but for other reasons. The switch from coal gas in homes for domestic use to coal gas was made for cost reasons. Natural gas became less expensive than coal gas. Car exhaust became less toxic in order to lessen environmental pollution. The reduction in suicides using these methods was incidental.

The major objections to making the required changes in order to prevent suicide are cost (car manufacturers resist making changes, claiming, erroneously, that it would cost too much) and esthetics (some argue that fencing in the Golden Gate Bridge in San Francisco spoils the esthetics of the bridge). In contrast, restricting access to firearms runs into extremely strong political opposition in the United States, but less so in other countries.

The present book will focus on research on preventing suicide by restricting access to firearms. It will not debate the political issues involved, nor interpretations of the Second Amendment. After all, if the research does not support this strategy for preventing suicide, the political issues become irrelevant. Of course, the arguments for restricting access to firearms (or particular types of firearms) in order to prevent murder and mass murder are a topic for another, different book.

## References

Clarke, R. V., & Lester, D. (1989). *Suicide: Closing the exits*. New York: Springer-Verlag.

Clarke, R. V., & Lester, D. (2013). *Suicide: Closing the exits*. New Brunswick, NJ: Transaction.

Lester, D. (2009). *Preventing suicide: Closing the exits revisited*. Hauppauge, NY: Nova Science Publishers, Inc.

In: Firearms and Suicide
Editor: David Lester
ISBN: 978-1-53614-690-5


*Chapter 1*

# Firearms, Suicide and Homicide: A Review

***David Lester, PhD*** [*]
Stockton University, Galloway, New Jersey, US

## Abstract

Since 1980, David Lester, the Author of this chapter, has produced an extensive body of research on firearms and handgun control. This chapter reviews this research, addressing four issues: (1) Do strict handgun control laws have a preventive impact on the use of guns for suicide and homicide, (2) Does the prevalence of firearm ownership impact the use of guns for suicide and homicide, (3) Do the regional and time-series social correlates of suicide and homicide differ for firearm suicide and firearm homicide rates as compared to the rates of suicide and homicide using other methods, and (4) Do people perceive the different methods for suicide differently? It will be shown that Lester's research suggests that the answer to each of these question is "Yes."

[*] Corresponding Author Email: lesterd@stockton.edu.

# Handgun Control, Suicide and Homicide

## Handgun Control Laws in the USA

Lester and Murrell (1980) studied Bakal's (1968) coding of the handgun control laws of the American states in 1968. They found that states with stricter handgun control laws had lower total suicide rates in 1959-1961 and in 1969-1971, lower male suicide rates, but not lower female suicide rates. They attributed this sex difference to the fact that, in 1960, 56% of male suicides used guns versus only 25% of female suicides. The association was also found for the suicide rate of all age groups (Lester, 1983).

Yang and Lester (1991) also found that the strictness of handgun control laws was negatively associated with the firearm suicide rate and the total suicide rate, suggesting that suicidal people do not switch to other methods for suicide if handguns are less available. The suicide rates by poisons and by hanging in 1970 were not significantly associated with the strictness of handgun control laws (Lester & Murrell, 1986; Lester, 1986), also indicating that, when handgun control laws were strict, suicidal individuals did not switch to the other popular methods for suicides.

Lester and Murrell (1982) followed up these studies by showing that states with stricter handgun control laws, while having lower suicide rates by gun, did have higher rates of suicide by "other means."[1] Lester (1987b) found that the impact of struct handgun controls on the use of firearms for suicide was found even after controls for church attendance. Lester and Murrell (1981c) found that the major influences on suicides using firearms were restrictions on the buyer and on the seller but not on carrying a firearm.

Lester and Murrell (1982, 1986) found that states with stricter handgun control laws had lower percentages of suicides and of homicide committed with firearms, but did not differ in their homicide rates using firearms.

For accidental deaths using guns, Lester and Murrell (1981b, 1986) found that states with stricter handgun controls laws had lower accidental death rates from guns in 1960 and 1970. However, the states with stricter

[1] "Other means" did not include poisons or hanging, but was the residual category after the major methods of suicide were taken into account.

handgun control laws also had lower accidental death rates from poisons and drowning, which could not have been impacted by handgun control laws, and had a greater increase in accidental death from guns from 1960 to 1970 which argues against a preventive effect. Lester (1993e) found that the age-adjusted firearm death rates (from suicide, homicide and accidents combined) for 1979-1987 was negatively associated with the strictness of handgun control laws. Lester and Murrell (1981a) found that, of 47 major cities, the cities in states with stricter handgun controls laws had higher homicide rates and a greater increase in the homicide rate from 1964 to 1972.

## Changes in Gun Control Laws in the USA

Lester (1988j) studied three states that strengthened their handgun control laws (MD in 1966, SC in 1973, and UT in 1973). The proportions of suicides using guns in the three-year periods before and after the change were examined. For two states (MD and UT), the proportion of suicides using guns rose, as did the proportion for the USA as a whole for the same periods. For one state (SC), the proportion dropped, whereas the proportion rose for the USA as a whole for the same period.

## Gun Control in Canada

Canada strengthened its gun control laws (Bill C-51) in 1977. Lester and Leenaars (1993, 1994) examined the period of 1969-1985 and found that the percentage of suicides using guns decreased after passage of the law, as did the firearm suicide rate. However, the suicide rate by all other methods increased suggesting that suicidal individuals switched methods for suicide. Leenaars and Lester (1994) found a similar effect for homicide. There was a decrease in the use of firearms for homicide (both the firearm homicide rate and the percentage of firearms used for homicide), but an increase in rate of homicide by all other methods and no change in the overall homicide rate. Leenaars and Lester (1996, 1999) found that this displacement of methods for suicide and homicide was found for men, but women showed no displacement of methods. Leenaars and Lester (1997) found that the impact of the gun control law on suicide was found only for those under the age of 65. For homicide, the preventive impact of the gun control law was found only for victims over the age of 55.

For the accidental death rate from firearms, Leenaars and Lester (1997b) found that the accidental death rate from firearms decreased for both men and for women after the passage of Bill C-51.

Lester (2000a) looked at the time-series rates for Canada for the period 1970-1996. The simple Pearson correlations indicated that the accidental death rate from firearms was positively associated with the firearm suicide rate (and not associated with the suicide rate by all other methods) and positively associated with the firearm homicide rate and negatively with the homicide rate by all other methods. An index of the percentage of suicides plus homicides by firearms was positively associated with the firearm suicide rate and negatively associated with the suicide rate by all other methods. This index was positively associated with the firearm homicide rate (but not associated with the homicide rate by all other methods).[2] For the period 1974-1990, Lester (2001b) found that the firearm accidental death rate was positively associated with the percentage of suicides and of homicide by firearm for all ages except suicides over the age of 55 and for homicide victims over the age of 55. Leenaars, et al. (2003) used more complex time series analyses to show that the passage of Bill C-51 had a preventive impact on both male and female firearm suicide rates, with evidence for displacement to other methods only for males. Controlling for social variables did not change these results markedly.

## Gun Ownership

Lester (1988f) found that the percentages of households with guns and the per capita ownership of guns in the six of the seven Australian states

[2] Lester (2000d) found that the firearm accidental death rate and the percentage of suicides plus homicide using firearms predicted the armed robbery rate using firearms over time from 1970-1995, and these two measures were negatively associated with rate of armed robbery using other methods.

(data from Northern Territories were incomplete) were positively associated with the percentage of suicides and of homicides using guns. Both of the gun ownership measures were positively associated with the firearm suicide rate and negatively with the suicide rate by all other methods. Both measures of gun ownership were positively associated with the total suicide rate, but not significantly so.

Lester (1988h, 1988i) replicated this Australian study using the nine major regions of the USA (rather than the 48 continental states). Several measures of gun ownership (% of suicides by firearm, % of homicides by firearms, accidental death rate from firearms, and subscriptions to firearm magazines [see below]) each significantly predicted the suicide rate by firearms and the homicide rate by firearms. The suicide rate by all methods other than firearms was higher in regions where indices of gun ownership were lower (suggesting switching of methods for suicide), whereas the homicide rate by all methods other than firearms was not consistently associated with indices of gun ownership.

Lester and Clarke (1991) examined gun ownership in the USA from 1959-1984, distinguishing between ownership of handguns, rifles and shotguns. The accidental death rate from firearms was positively associated over time with ownership of shotguns and negatively with ownership of handguns. The firearm suicide rate was positively associated with ownership of handguns and negatively with ownership of shotguns, whereas the firearm homicide rate was positively associated with ownership of handguns and rifles and negatively with ownership of shotguns.

For 12 nations with direct measures of household gun ownership, Lester (1996b) found that this measure was positively associated with the percentage of suicides using guns, the accidental death rate from firearms and the firearm suicide rate (but not the suicide rate by all other methods). Household gun ownership was positively associated with the firearm homicide rate, but also with the homicide rate by all other methods (and not significantly with the percentage of homicides using firearms). For these 12 nations, Lester (1999) found that the percentage of households with guns was positively associated with the total death rate from firearms in children aged 0-15, overall and for firearm deaths from suicide, homicide and accidental. Similar associations were found the percentage of suicides in the nation by firearm and the percentage of homicide in the nations by firearm.

## Percentage of Homicides and Suicides Using Guns

Lester (1987a) found that the percentage of homicides using guns (a measure of the distribution of guns in a region) in the American states in 1970 was positively associated the firearm suicide rate, negatively with the suicide rate by all other methods and not associated with the total suicide rate. For 38 states with available data, Lester (2005) found that the firearm death rate for children and adolescents was associated with measures of firearm prevalence and handgun control law strictness. For 28 states, reports by high school youths of whether they had carried a gun in the past 30 days were also associated with gun prevalence, handgun control strictness and the youth firearm mortality rate.

Lester (1994b) found that the percentage of suicides using firearms in the 48 continental states was associated with social disintegration (e.g., divorce and migration rates), an index of southernness, Roman Catholicism, urban residence/wealth, and age. The percentage of homicides using firearms was associated with southernness, Roman Catholicism, and urban residence/wealth.

In a study of 20 countries, Lester (1990a) found that the percentage of homicides using guns was positively associated with the firearm suicide rate and negatively with the suicide rate by all other methods. Similar results were obtained for an index using the percentage of suicides using guns.

Lester (1991a) found that, for 16 European nations, the percentage of suicides using firearms and the accidental death rate from firearms were positively associated. Both of these measures were positively associated with the firearm homicide rate, but not with the homicide rate using other methods. Lester (2000c) extended these analyses to 36 nations and found that the percentage of homicides using firearms was associated positively with the firearm suicide rate and negatively with the suicide rate by all other methods. The associations for the accidental firearm death rate were not statistically significant (although positively associated with the firearm suicide rate). Both the accidental firearm death rate and the percentage of suicides using firearms were positively associated with the firearm homicide rate.

For the eight largest Canadian provinces, the percentage of homicides using firearms in 1980 was not associated with the percentage of suicides using firearms or the firearm suicide rate (Lester, 1994d). For the 12 regions of Canada (ten provinces and two territories), Lester and Leenaars (1998) found that the accidental death rate from firearms was positively associated with the total suicide rate, the firearm suicide rate and the non-firearm suicide rate (with the first two correlations statistically significant). The same pattern was found for the total homicide rate, the firearm homicide rate and the non-firearm suicide rate, with all three correlations statistically significant. The percentage of homicides committed with firearms was positively associated with the total suicide rate (not significantly) and the firearm suicide rate (significantly), and negatively with the non-firearm suicide rate (not significantly).

For the 12 regions of Canada (ten provinces and two territories), Lester and Leenaars (1998) found inconsistent associations between the accidental death rate from firearms, the firearm suicide rate and the firearm homicide rate, and the percentages of suicides and of homicide using firearms. Eleven of the 12 correlations were positive, but only four of these correlations were statistically significant. Whereas the suicide rate showed (non-significant) evidence of switching, the homicide rate did not.

## Accidental Death Rate from Guns

Lester (1987a, 1989d, 1993c) found that the accidental death rate using guns (a measure of the distribution of guns in a region) in the American states in 1970 and in 1977-1979 was positively associated the firearm suicide rate,[3] negatively with the suicide rate by all other methods (but not significantly) and not significantly associated with the total suicide rate.[4]

For the eight largest Canadian provinces, the accidental death rate from firearms in 1980 was positively associated with the percentage of suicides using firearms and the firearm suicide rate but negatively with the suicide rate by all other methods (Lester, 1994d).

For 17 nations in 1980, Lester (1993d, 1994c) found that the accidental death rate for firearms was positively associated with the percentages of suicides using firearms and the percentages of homicides using firearms.

## Firearm Death Rates

Lester (2001a) found that the death rate from firearms in general in the 48 continental states of the USA in 1979-1987 was positively with the associated the percentage of residents in poverty and negatively with the physicians per capita (but not with the hospital beds per capita). The total firearm death rate was also associated positively with indices of social disintegration (e.g., divorce) and an index of southernness and negatively with female labor force participation.

## Subscriptions to Firearm Magazines

Since it is difficult to get accurate estimates of firearm ownership by region in the USA, Lester (1989c) used the circulation in 1980 of three magazines for owners of firearms (*Shooting Times*, *Guns and Ammo*, and *American Handgunner*). States with a higher per capita circulation of the three magazines had higher firearm suicide rates, but no different suicide

---

[3] But not over the ten age groups in 1977-1979.

[4] Lester (1990e) showed that this measure, while useful for regional studies, may not be valid for time-series studies. From 1950-1984 in the USA, the accidental death rate from firearms and the firearm suicide rate were negatively associated. However, these two measures were positively associated in Japan from 1950 to 1980 where, however, firearm ownership is much less common than in the USA (Lester, 1990f).

rates by all other methods. The total suicide rate was higher in states with higher firearm magazine circulation rates. The results for homicides showed no significant associations. Lester (1993e) replicated these results using age-adjusted firearm deaths rates (from suicide, homicide and accidents combined) for 1979-1987, but the correlation was significant only for *Shooting Times*.

## Hunting Licenses

Lester (1995) looked at the per capita purchase of hunting licenses in the 48 continental states in 1980. This measure was positively associated with the sales of firearms magazines, the strictness of state handgun control laws, and the firearm suicide rate, but not with the suicide rate by all other methods. The measure was *negatively* associated with the firearm homicide rate as well as the homicide rate by all other methods.

## Firearm Dealers

Lester (1993b) found that the per capita density of firearms dealers in 1990 in the 48 continental states of the USA was not associated with the age-adjusted firearms suicide rate for 1979-1987.

## Changes over Time

Lester (1991c) found that different measures of gun ownership from 1967 to 1983 were not associated. Three clusters emerged: (i) estimates of gun ownership, (ii) percentage of guns used for homicide, and (iii) percentage of guns used for suicide and subscriptions to gun magazines. Yang and Lester (1989) found that changes in the percentage of households owning handguns from year to year for the period 1959-1984 was not associated with changes in the percentage of suicides using handguns, or changes in the suicide rate using firearms.

### Primary versus Secondary Murder

Lester (1985) found that states with stricter handgun control laws did not have higher (or lower) rates of primary homicide (where the murderer and victim know each other) but did have higher rates of non-primary homicide, the opposite of a preventive effect. Lester (1990c) found that the percentage of suicides using firearms and the accidental death rate from firearms in the 48 continental states in 1973 was positively associated with the rate of primary murder (involving family and friends) in 1970 but not with the rate of secondary murder (involving strangers).

### The Murder of Police Officers

Lester (1984) found that the rate with police officers were murdered in 57 American cities was positively associated with several measures of gun ownership (% suicides by firearm, % homicides by firearm, and the accidental death rate by firearms), but not the strictness of handgun control law of the state in which the city lay.

## Other Issues

### The Perception of Different Methods for Suicide

Lester (1988b) asked undergraduate students to rate 11 methods for suicide as acceptable on a scale of 1 to 5. Sleeping pills/antidepressants was rated as most acceptable (mean rating 4.1) followed by car exhaust (2.5). All other methods, including guns, had ratings less than 2.

Lester (1988a) asked undergraduates to state whether they would choose a gun or an overdose of pills as a method for suicide (26% chose a gun). They then rated each of these two methods on the dimensions of quick-slow, painful-painless, difficult-easy, irreversible-reversible, good-bad, courageous-cowardly, dramatic-banal, masculine-feminine, messy-tidy and impulsive-planned. Suicide by guns was viewed as quick, painful, difficult, irreversible, dramatic, masculine, messy, courageous, and impulsive, whereas suicide using pills was viewed as slow, painless, easy, cowardly, feminine, tidy and planned. Men and women did not differ in their ratings of guns

Lester (1988c) asked undergraduates which method they would choose for suicide, and whether they chose that method because it was quick, painless, not disfiguring and easily available. Women chose an overdose of pills more than did men, while men chose a gun more than did women. Women rated availability, painlessness and less disfigurement as more important reasons for their choice of method than did men. Those choosing a gun viewed quickness as an important reason for their choice and disfigurement as less important, and they also showed less concern (on a fear of the consequences of death scale) with what would happen to their body after death. Lester (1979) found no differences in the fears of death and dying between undergraduates who would choose guns or hanging for suicide and those who would choose drugs.

The problem with this type of research is that the researcher provides the constructs to be rated. Lester (1993a) gave undergraduates eight methods of suicide and asked them to provide their own eight constructs on which to rate them (using a yes-no answer format). Each 8x8 grid was unique, and Lester suggested that this might be useful information for a therapist to have about a client. Interestingly, the 28 students used many of the same constructs that Lester had used in his earlier studies (such as masculine, bloody/messy and certainty of outcome), but there were also different constructs suggested by the students (e.g., needs skill, noisy, unusual, and active/aggressive).

Lester (1988d) gave undergraduates a case study of an alcoholic and depressed faculty member who died by suicide, either by gunshot or by an overdose of pills. The method of suicide did not affect the evaluation (on a scale of 1-10) of the suicide's level of psychiatric disturbance.

## Sex Differences in the Use of Guns for Suicide

In the USA, men use guns for suicide more than do women, but this difference varies by state. Using data from 1980, Lester (1992) found that both women and men used guns for suicide more in the southern and western states, and the difference in the percentage of women and men using guns for suicide was less in states where guns are used more for suicide.

Heim and Lester (1991) found that firearms were not used very often for suicide in West Berlin for the period 1981-1985 (3.4%), but 93.3% of these firearm suicides were male. For 25 nations in 1980, Lester (1994a) found that men and women did not differ in their suicide rate using solids/liquids, but that men had higher suicide rates by all other methods, including firearms. The question, therefore, may be, not why do men have higher suicide rates than women (as they do in almost all countries), but rather why do men have higher *violent suicide rates* than women.

## Types of Firearm

Lester and Frank (1988) found limited data from 1980 on the type of gun used by suicides. Data were available for only 33% of suicides, for whom 13.7% used handguns, 12.8% shotguns and 6.6% rifles. States with stricter handgun control laws had a lower percentage of suicides using handguns versus long guns. Handguns were used relatively more often by women, nonwhites and those aged more than 25, while single individuals used handguns relatively less often. Lester (1998) found that the percentage of murders committed with long guns (versus handguns) was higher in states which were more rural and in which more hunting licenses per capita were issued.

## The Suicide Notes of those Using Firearms

There has been very little research on the personality of those choosing different methods for suicide, although Lester (1988e) found no differences in the MMPI scores of those using firearms and those using overdoses for suicide.

Lester (1970a, 1970b) compared those using active methods for suicide (which includes firearms as wells as hanging and jumping) with those using passive methods and found no difference on the Thematic Apperception Test or on the MMPI. Those who used firearms were younger than those using hanging, but the two groups did not differ in MMPI scores. Lester, et al. (1976) compared completed suicides who used drugs, hanging and firearms and found that men used firearms and hanging more than did women. Those using hanging were older, while those using firearms were more often African-American. Those using firearms were more often single and living alone, were less likely to have abused drugs or been psychiatrically hospitalized in the past, and less often had previously attempted suicide. They did not differ on an objective measure of suicide intent based on the circumstances of the suicidal act, in the use of alcohol during the suicidal act, leaving a suicide note, history of depression, or recent stressors.

There has been some research on the suicide notes of those who choose firearms for suicide. Lester (1971a, 1971b) failed to find differences in the content of suicide notes of those using violent versus non-violent methods for suicide. Lester (2014; Lester, Haines & Williams, 2010) reported analyses of the content of suicide notes by the method used for suicide. In a small sample of American suicide notes, only two differences were found between those using pills (n = 19) and those using firearms (n = 15): those using firearms scored lower on the use of words concerned with discrepancies (such as *would*, *should* and *could*), and somewhat more focus on words connected with causation (Lester, 2014). In a large sample of Australian suicide notes (Lester, et al., 2010), those using firearms (n = 98), as compared to those using solids and liquids (n = 63) and those using gas (n = 42), had a lower percentage of words concerned with sadness/depression and fewest future tense verbs. Those using gas had more references to friends, words concerned with "down," exclusion words (such as *but* and *except*), occupation and achievement. Those using solids and liquids had the most references to sadness/depression and the most future tense verbs. This suggests that those using guns may be in an acute crisis (and perhaps acting impulsively), whereas those using solids and liquids may more often have a chronic psychiatric condition.

In a study of Australia men, Lester, Haines and Williams (2012) found that those using firearms were younger, had more often ingested alcohol prior to the act, were less likely to have attempted suicide in the past, were more likely to leave a suicide note, were more likely to have visited a physician or psychiatrist in the recent months, were more often angry and less often sad (as confirmed by those who did leave suicide notes), depressed or withdrawn, and were more often reacting to interpersonal conflict and less often reacting to other stressful life events. Thus, these firearm suicides do seem to be more impulsive and not connected with psychiatric disorder;

## Social Correlates of Firearm Rates of Suicide and Homicide

In a study of the 48 continental states of the USA in 1980, Lester (1990b) found that scores for seven clusters of variables (factors), identified in a factor analysis of 37 socio-economic variables, were associated differently with the suicide rate using each method for suicide. For example, scores for a factor assessing social integration (e.g., divorce rate and interstate migration) were associated (positively) only with the suicide rates by firearms and by solids/liquids. States with a higher southernness index and higher church attendance had lower rates of suicide by hanging and gases. These results suggested that suicides by each method may be different phenomena, requiring different explanations. Lester (1997) found that the murder rates by each method also had different social correlates. The firearm murder rate was associated with an index of southernness and participation in the labor force, but not with factors such as urban location/wealth or social disintegration (e.g., divorce and interstate migration rates).

Lester (1991b), using a small sample of 13 European nations, found that the firearm suicide rate was not associated with the divorce rate, whereas the suicide rates using solids/liquids, gas, drowning and cutting were associated with the divorce rate.

Over time for the period 1950-1985 in the USA, Lester (2000b) found that the social correlates of suicide rates varied with the method used for suicide. The firearm suicide rate was associated with the divorce rate (positively) and with marriage and birth rates (negatively), correlates which differed from those obtained for the suicide rates by solids/liquids and by hanging. The social correlates of firearm homicide rates were similar to the social correlates for the homicide rate using other methods (positively with divorce rates).

Lester (1996a) found that the social correlates of the rates of suicide and homicide committed by different methods over time in England and Wales from 1950-1985 varied by method. For example, the rate of suicide using firearms (and of homicide using firearms) was not associated with marriage, birth, divorce or unemployment rates, whereas suicide rates using car exhaust was positively associated with divorce and unemployment rates (as Durkheim's [1897] theory would predict). Homicide rates using cutting were positively associated with divorce rates and negatively with unemployment rates.

Lester and Abe (1998) found that predictors of the Japanese suicide rate for the period 1970-1989 also varied by the method used for suicide. The firearm suicide rate was predicted by the birth rate (positively) and the marriage rate (negatively). The suicide rate by hanging was predicted only by the divorce rate (positively).

## Opportunity-Based Suicide Rates

Lester (1988g) suggested that *opportunity-based suicide rates* may be more meaningful than traditional suicide rates. For example, the firearm suicide rate in the USA in 1979 was 6.87 per 100,000 people per year versus 9.38 per 100,000 guns per year. Lester (1990d) showed that the social correlates of firearm opportunity-based suicide rates were somewhat different over the nine regions of the USA than the social correlates of simple firearm suicide rates. For example, firearm opportunity-based suicide rates were positively associated with the percentage of urban population in the regions, whereas the firearm suicide rates were negatively associated with the percentage of urban population in the regions.

## LIMITATIONS

There are several limitations to the research reviewed here.

### Gun Control Laws

The research on gun control in the USA was limited to the handgun control laws coded by Bakal (1968). An analysis of gun control laws in general was not available. In a study of deaths from firearms in May 1-7, 1989, only 63% of the suicides and 77% of homicides used handguns (Lester, 1989a). There were no differences in age and sex in those using handguns and those using long guns for suicide. For Canada, however, it was possible to analyze the impact of a particular gun control law (Bill C-51) on the use of guns from suicide and homicide. Future research should explore firearm control laws in the states of the USA covering all guns and also changes after gun control laws are modified, both at the state level and at the federal level.

### Gun Ownership

The research is limited by the lack of comprehensive measures of gun ownership. Occasionally, rough measures are published, but the research reported in this chapter often had to rely on proxy measures: the percentages of suicides and of homicides using guns, the accidental death rate from firearms, the circulation of firearm magazines, the density of firearms dealers, and the per capita issue of hunting licenses. Future research would benefit from more accurate and comprehensive measures of firearm ownership.

## Switching

One important issue is whether people would switch methods for suicide if their preferred method were unavailable. There is very little research on the frequency with which suicidal individuals do switch methods for their suicidal behavior. Lester (1989b) compared undergraduates who rated pills as very acceptable for suicide and those who rated firearms as very acceptable for how acceptable they found other methods of suicide. Those choosing firearms rated other methods as more acceptable than those choosing pills, suggesting that they would be more likely to switch methods if guns were unavailable. Lester, et al. (1989) studied psychiatric inpatients with a history of attempted suicide. Of those who had made two or more attempts, 32% switched methods. Those who switched methods did not differ in sex, age, race or marital status from those who did not switch, but were less likely to be diagnosed as schizophrenic. It seems that a fair proportion of suicidal individuals do switch methods, but not all do so. More research is needed on the extent to which people switch methods for suicides if they make multiple suicide attempts, and that factors are associated with switching methods for suicide.

Studies of suicides using firearms versus those using other methods suggested that there are differences in these two groups of individuals. Those using firearms seem to be less psychiatrically disturbed, more angry, and more impulsive. Since the use of a firearms for suicide and for homicide is accomplished very quickly, whereas other methods take more time to cause death, access to firearms will make it possible for angry and impulsive individuals to kill themselves or others more easily.

## Conclusion

This chapter addressed four questions. First, do strict handgun control laws have a preventive impact on the use of guns for suicide and homicide and does the prevalence of firearm ownership impact the use of guns for suicide and homicide. The research reviewed in this chapter does seem to indicate that reduced access to guns does result in lower rates of firearm suicide, firearm homicide and accidental death rates from firearms. However, the majority of the studies (9 studies out of 12) showed switching, that is, the less often guns are used for suicide the more often other methods are used. Although occasional studies show that reduced access to guns is associated with lower *total rates of suicide* and of homicide, the results are not consistent. However, there evidence from one study in Canada that evidence for the switching of methods for suicide was found only in men and not in women.

Looking at the possibilities for preventing suicide in particular, since the use of firearms for suicide does result in a quick death, there is less opportunity for the suicidal individual to change his or her mind and call for help (either at a suicide prevention or crisis intervention center or for medical help). At the individual level, it is easy to find cases of people changing their minds and seeking help after taking medications or of others intervening to stop the people from dying. Therefore, even if people do switch methods for suicide, if they switch from a more lethal method to a less lethal methods, lives ay be saved.

The third question was whether the regional and time-series social correlates of suicide and homicide differ for firearm suicide and firearm homicide as compared to the rates of suicide and homicide using other methods. The answer here is that they do. This does suggest that theories of suicide may need to be modified to be theories of a particular method for suicide. A *general* theory of suicide (or of homicide) may be inadequate to explain the phenomena.

The final question was whether people perceive the different methods for suicide differently? The answer is that they do and this, of course, may affect their choice of method for suicide. However, the research reviewed was conducted on samples of undergraduate students, and future research should be conducted on suicidal individuals.

## Proposals

As noted above, future research of the relationship between firearms and suicide requires

1. A more detailed analysis of particular aspects of the laws related to gun control. As will be seen in the next chapter (Chapter 2), other researchers have recently addressed this issue.
2. The differences found for the use of handguns versus long guns (rifles and shotguns) suggests that a much more detailed description and analysis of the guns used by suicides would be useful, as well as when and where the individuals obtained access to or purchased those guns.
3. More research is needed on the personality and social characteristics of those choosing guns for suicide. We know that guns are used for suicide more by men than by women, and more in rural areas than in urban areas. These is some evidence that those who choose guns for suicide may be more impulsive and less psychiatrically disturbed. More information on this might provide clues for psychotherapists and counselors whose clients may be suicidal.
4. Undergraduate students viewed the use of firearms for suicide as painful, difficult, and messy. Lester (1989e) noted that public education regarding suicide was very different than that for cancer and, most recently, opioid addiction. These latter ads are dramatic, difficult to watch yet powerful. I have always thought that the television ad of Yul Brunner arguing against smoking which aired after he had died of lung cancer was incredibly moving. Media ads for suicide prevention have always taken a different route, focusing on seeking help and de-stigmatizing the behavior. Understanding the personality and psychodynamics of those choosing different

methods for suicide may provide clues on how to focus public education programs and advertisements.[5]

## References

Bakal, C. (1968). *No right to bear arms*. New York: Paperback Library.

Durkheim, E. (1897). *Le suicide*. Paris, France: Felix Alcan.

Heim, N. & Lester, D. (1991). Factors affecting choice of method for suicide. *European Journal of Psychiatry*, *5*, 161-165.

Leenaars, A. A. & Lester, D. (1994). Effects of gun control on homicide in Canada. *Psychological Reports*, *75*, 81-82.

Leenaars, A. A. & Lester, D. (1996). Gender and the impact of gun control on suicide and homicide. *Archives of Suicide Research*, *2*, 223-234.

Leenaars, A. A. & Lester, D. (1997a). The impact of gun control on suicide and homicide across the life span. *Canadian Journal of Behavioural Science*, *29*(1), 1-6.

Leenaars, A. A. & Lester, D. (1997b). The effects of gun control of the accidental death rate from firearms in Canada. *Journal of Safety Research*, *28*, 119-122.

Leenaars, A. A. & Lester, D. (1999). Gender, gun control, suicide and homicide. *Archives of Suicide Research*, *5*, 77-79.

Leenaars, A. A., Moksony, F., Lester, D. & Wenckstern, S. (2003). The impact of gun control (Bill C-51) on suicide in Canada. *Death Studies*, *27*, 103-124.

Lester, D. (1970a). Personality correlates associated with choice of method of committing suicide. *Personality*, *1*, 261-264.

Lester, D. (1970b). Factors affecting choice of method of suicide. *Journal of Clinical Psychology*, *26*, 437.

[5] In the days when I was working at the Suicide Prevention and Crisis Intervention Center in Buffalo, New York (1969-1971), we considered whether running ads (on transport buses, the radio and television) advertising the availability of our telephone crisis services would be counter-productive and incite suicidal behavior. There was no way to empirically examine whether our concern was justified, but we did worry.

Lester, D. (1971a). Need for affiliation in suicide notes. *Perceptual & Motor Skills*, *33*, 550.

Lester, D. (1971b). Choice of method for suicide and personality. *Omega*, *2*, 76-80.

Lester, D. (1979). Preference for method of suicide and attitudes toward death in normal people. *Psychological Reports*, *45*, 638.

Lester, D. (1983). Preventive effect of strict handgun control laws on suicide rates. *American Journal of Psychiatry*, *140*, 1259.

Lester, D. (1984). The murder of police officers in American cities. *Criminal Justice & Behavior*, *11*, 101-113.

Lester, D. (1985). Handgun control laws, suicide and homicide. *American Journal of Psychiatry*, *142*, 144.

Lester, D. (1987a). Availability of guns and the likelihood of suicide. *Sociology & Social Research*, *71*, 287-288.

Lester, D. (1987b). An availability-acceptability theory of suicide. *Activitas Nervosa Superior*, *29*, 164-166.

Lester, D. (1988a). The perception of different methods of suicide. *Journal of General Psychology*, *115*, 215-217.

Lester, D. (1988b). The perception of different methods for suicide. *Perceptual & Motor Skills*, *76*, 530.

Lester, D. (1988c). Why do people choose particular methods for suicide? *Activitas Nervosa Superior*, *30*, 312-314.

Lester, D. (1988d). Effect of method of suicide on the perception of the suicidal person. *Perceptual & Motor Skills*, *66*, 578.

Lester, D. (1988e). Excitor-inhibitor scales of the MMPI and choice of method for suicide. *Perceptual & Motor Skills*, *66*, 218.

Lester, D. (1988f). Restricting the availability of guns as a strategy for preventing suicide. *Biology & Society*, *5*, 127-129.

Lester, D. (1988g). Opportunity-based suicide rates. *Psychological Reports*, *63*, 984.

Lester, D. (1988h). Firearm availability and the incidence of suicide and homicide. *Acta Psychiatrica Belgica*, *88*, 387-393.

Lester, D. (1988i). Gun control, gun ownership, and suicide prevention. *Suicide & Life-Threatening Behavior*, *18*, 176-180.

Lester, D. (1988j). Effect of changes in handgun control laws on suicide rates. *Psychological Reports*, *62*, 298.

Lester, D. (1989a). Use of handguns and long guns in suicide and homicide. *Psychological Reports*, *65*, 938.

Lester, D. (1989b). Are those who choose guns for suicide more intent on dying? *Perceptual & Motor Skills*, *69*, 922.

Lester, D. (1989c). Gun ownership and suicide in the United States. *Psychological Medicine*, *19*, 519-521.

Lester, D. (1989d). Specific agents of accidental and suicidal death. *Sociology & Social Research*, *73*, 182-184.

Lester, D. (1989e). Public health education against suicide. *Crisis*, *10*, 181-183.

Lester, D. (1990a). The availability of firearms and the use of firearms for suicide. *Acta Psychiatric Scandinavica*, *81*, 146-147.

Lester, D. (1990b). The regional variation of suicide by different methods. *Crisis*, *11*, 32-37.

Lester, D. (1990c). Relationship between firearm availability and primary and secondary murder. *Psychological Reports*, *67*, 490.

Lester, D. (1990d). A study of opportunity-based suicide rates. *Psychological Reports*, *67*, 498.

Lester, D. (1990e). Accidental death rates and suicide. *Activitas Nervosa Superior*, *32*, 130-131.

Lester, D. (1990f). The availability of lethal methods for suicide and the suicide rate. *Stress Medicine*, *6*, 275-276.

Lester, D. (1991a). Crime as opportunity. *British Journal of Criminology*, *31*, 186-188.

Lester, D. (1991b). Are the social correlates of suicide and homicide rates the same for each lethal weapon? *European Journal of Psychiatry*, *8*, 5-8.

Lester, D. (1991c). Association of different measures of gun ownership over time. *Psychological Reports*, *69*, 1058.

Lester, D. (1992). Sex differences in the methods used for suicide. *Psychological Reports*, *71*, 1234.

Lester, D. (1993a). How do people perceive the different methods for suicide. *Death Studies*, *17*, 179-184.

Lester, D. (1993b). Firearm deaths and the density of firearms dealers in America. *Perceptual & Motor Skills*, *76*, 978.

Lester, D. (1993c). Availability of methods for suicide and suicide rates. *Perceptual & Motor Skills*, *76*, 1358.

Lester, D. (1993d). Firearm availability and accidental deaths from firearms. *Journal of Safety Research*, *24*, 167-169.

Lester, D. (1993e). Firearms deaths in the United States and gun availability. *American Journal of Public Health*, *83*, 1642.

Lester, D. (1994a). Sex differences in methods for suicide. *Perceptual & Motor Skills*, *79*, 418.

Lester, D. (1994b). Social correlates of the percentage of suicides and homicides employing firearms. *Perceptual & Motor Skills*, *79*, 254,

Lester, D. (1994c). Are suicides disguised as accidental and undetermined deaths? *European Journal of Psychiatry*, *8*, 89-92.

Lester, D. (1994d). Use of firearms for suicide in Canada. *Perceptual & Motor Skills*, *79*, 962.

Lester, D. (1995). The availability of guns and the rates of personal violence (homicide and suicide). *Italian Journal of Suicidology*, *5*, 73-76.

Lester, D. (1996a). Are murders and suicides committed by different methods intrinsically different? *Medicine, Science & the Law*, *36*, 28-30.

Lester, D. (1996b). Gun ownership and rates of homicide and suicide. *European Journal of Psychiatry*, *10*, 83-85.

Lester, D. (1997). Social correlates of murder rates by each method. *Perceptual & Motor Skills*, *85*, 1314.

Lester, D. (1998). The use of long guns for murder. *Perceptual & Motor Skills*, *87*, 162.

Lester, D. (1999). Gun deaths in children and guns in the home. *European Journal of Psychiatry*, *13*, 157-159.

Lester, D. (2000a). Gun availability and the use of guns for suicide and homicide in Canada. *Canadian Journal of Public Health*, *91*, 186-187.

Lester, D. (2000b). Correlates of rates of suicide and homicide committed by different methods. *Perceptual & Motor Skills*, *91*, 616.

Lester, D. (2000c). Firearm availability and the use of firearms for suicide and homicide. *Perceptual & Motor Skills*, *91*, 998.

Lester, D. (2000d). Armed robbery and the availability of firearms in Canada. *Euro Criminology*, *14*, 113-115.

Lester, D. (2001a). Social correlates of injury mortality rates. *Advances in Psychology Research*, *3*, 235-244.

Lester, D. (2001b). Gun availability and use of guns for murder and suicide in Canada. *Psychological Reports*, *89*, 624.

Lester, D. (2005). Association of gun related measures in American states and child and adolescent firearm mortality. *Psychological Reports*, *97*, 757-758.

Lester, D. (2014). *The "I" of the storm*. Berlin, Germany: De Gruyter.

Lester, D. & Abe, K. (1998). The suicide rate by each method in Japan. *Archives of Suicide Research*, *4*, 281-285.

Lester, D., Beck, A. T. & Bruno, S. (1976). Correlates of choice of method for completed suicide. *Psychology*, *13*(2), 70-73.

Lester, D. & Clarke, R. V. (1991). Note on "Suicide and increased availability of handguns in the United States." *Social Science & Medicine*, *32*, 1311-1313.

Lester, D., Fong, C. A. & D'Angelo, A. A. (1989). Chronic suicide attempters who switch methods and those who do not. *Perceptual & Motor Skills*, *69*, 1390.

Lester, D. & Frank, M. L. (1988). Handguns, long guns, and suicide. *Psychological Reports*, *63*, 606.

Lester, D., Haines, J. & Williams, C. (2010). Content differences in suicide notes by sex, age, and method. *Psychological Reports*, *106*, 475-476.

Lester, D., Haines, J. & Williams, C. (2012). Firearms suicides among males in Australia. *Internal Journal of Men's Health*, *11*, 170-176.

Lester, D. & Leenaars, A. (1993). Suicide rates in Canada before and after tightening firearm control laws. *Psychological Reports*, *72*, 787-790.

Lester, D. & Leenaars, A. A. (1994). Gun control and rates of firearms violence in Canada and the United States. *Canadian Journal of Criminology*, *36*, 463-464.

Lester, D. & Leenaars, A. A. (1998). Is there a regional subculture of firearm violence in Canada? *Medicine, Science & the Law*, *38*, 317-320.

Lester, D. & Murrell, M. E. (1980). The influence of gun control laws on suicidal behavior. *American Journal of Psychiatry*, *137*, 121-122.

Lester, D. & Murrell, M. E. (1981a). The relationship between gun control statutes and homicide rates: a research note. *Journal of Crime & Justice*, *4*, 145-148.

Lester, D. & Murrell, M. E. (1981b). The influence of gun control laws on the incidence of accidents with guns. *Accident Analysis & Prevention*, *13*, 357-359.

Lester, D. & Murrell, M. (1981c). The influence of strict handgun control laws on suicidal behavior in the U.S.A. In J. P. Soubrier & J. Vendrinne (Eds.) *Depression et suicide*, pp. 305-209. Paris, France: Pergamon.

Lester, D. & Murrell, M. (1982). The preventive effect of strict gun control laws on suicide and homicide. *Suicide & Life-Threatening Behavior*, *12*, 131-140.

Lester, D. & Murrell, M. (1986). The influence of gun control laws on personal violence. *Journal of Community Psychology*, *14*, 315-318.

Yang, B. & Lester, D. (1989). Suicide rates and handgun ownership in the United States 1959-1984. *Social Science & Medicine*, *29*, 1143.

Yang, B. & Lester, D. (1991). The effect of gun availability on suicide rates. *Atlantic Economic Journal*, *19*(2), 74.

In: Firearms and Suicide
Editor: David Lester

ISBN: 978-1-53614-690-5


*Chapter 2*

# SUICIDE AND FIREARMS: RESEARCH IN THE 20$^{TH}$ AND 21$^{ST}$ CENTURIES

***David Lester, PhD*** *

Stockton University, Galloway, New Jersey, US

## ABSTRACT

The work of David Lester on firearms and suicide was reviewed in Chapter 1. The present chapter reviews the research by others and draws conclusions from this impressive body of research.

The present chapter reviews the research of other scholars on the role of firearms in suicidal behavior. For this, I used all references with guns or firearms in the title in PsycInfo. The review is, therefore, not exhaustive, for I did not use other compilations of scholarly articles such as Criminal Justice Abstracts, Sociological Abstracts or PubMed. I also did not look at books on the topic, chapters in books or the reference lists in the articles that I did read. However, the articles were all in peer-reviewed scholarly journals and constitute the major research on firearms and suicide.

* Corresponding Author Email: lesterd@stockton.edu.

## Gun Control Legislation

Medoff and Magaddino (1983) examined two firearm control policies in the American states in 1970: a license to purchase and a waiting period. States with either provision had lower suicides rates, specifically for white males aged 20-64. A similar result was found comparing the six states rated by the NRA as having the most restrictive gun control laws with other states.

Boor and Bair (1990) found that eight elements of state gun control statutes in the United States in 1985 were associated with the state suicide rates. In a multiple regression with control variables, the predictors of the state suicide rates were the divorce rate, the crime rate, restrictions on sellers and restrictions on buyers.

Loftin, et al. (1991) found that passage of a strict handgun law in 1976 in Washington, DC, led to a drop of 23% in suicides using firearms but no change in other methods and no change in the neighboring states of Maryland and Virginia. Similar results were found for homicides.

Ludwig and Cook (2000) examined the impact of the passage of the Brady Handgun Violence Prevention Act in 1994 on suicides and homicide is the United States. States which implemented the changes (waiting periods and background checks) were compared with states that already had these restrictions. The only significant change was a decrease in firearm suicides among those over the age of 55, and this change was greater if both waiting periods and background checks were instituted rather than only background checks.

Crifasi, et al. (2015) examined the impact of a permit-to-purchase law in Connecticut and Missouri. Connecticut introduced such a law and saw a 15.4% reduction in the firearm suicide rate.[6] Missouri repealed such a law and saw a 16.1% increase in the firearm suicide rate. The presentation of data in this study is far from clear, but it appears that the non-firearm suicide rate in Connecticut did not increase markedly after the passage of the law, although a slight uptick can be noticed after eight years. In Missouri, repeal

[6] The effect was strongest in those aged 20-29.

of the law was followed by increases in both the firearm and non-firearm suicide rates.

Anestis, Khaem, Law, et al. (2015) studied the impact of three state laws (permit to purchase a handgun, registration of handguns, license to own a handgun) on suicide rates in 2010. States with any of these three laws had lower firearm suicide rates and lower overall suicide rates, indicating no switching of methods when handgun laws were in place, as well as a lower percentage of suicides using firearms. Anestis and Anestis (2015) studied the impact of four handgun laws (waiting periods, universal background checks, gun locks, and open carrying regulations) on suicide rates. All were associated with lower firearms suicide rates, and all were associated with a lower total suicide rate, except that the association for a waiting period was not statistically significant. Anestis, Anestis and Butterworth (2017) looked at changes in state suicide rates from 2013 to 2014 and found that mandatory waiting periods and universal background checks (but not open-carry restrictions or gun locks) were associated with decreases in overall suicide rates.

Anestis and Capron (2016) found that the state population of veterans (per 100,000) was positively associated with the statewide suicide rate, firearm suicide rate and the percentage of suicides using firearms, and also with a lack of state handgun laws. Anestis and Carpron speculated that veterans may impact statewide suicide rates because of their prior experience with firearms. Their tendency to live in states without handgun legislation may also exacerbate this phenomenon

Andres and Hempstead (2011) examined the impact of permit requirements, sales to minors, psychiatric/behavioral prohibitions, and criminal history prohibitions on the male suicide rate of the states. Although the results varied with age, permit requirements and restrictions on sales to minors had a preventive impact on male suicide rates. The effect of psychiatric/behavior and criminal history restrictions had a lesser impact, and many of the regression coefficients were not statistically significant. For the suicide rate of 15-24 year-old males, only permit requirements and restrictions on sales to minors had a preventive impact, while for the suicide rate of men over the age of 65, permit requirements and restrictions for alcohol abuse had a preventive impact.

Slater (2011) found that the overall suicide rate and the firearm suicide in the states of America were predicted by the leniency of state gun laws (in the year 2001), divorce rates and percentage of males. Political conservatism, economic climate and violence climate in the states were indirect predictors.

For the year 1999, Price, et al. (2004) found that the age-adjusted firearm suicide rate of the states was positively associated with the rate of firearm dealers per 100,000, and the ownership of firearms (as measured by the proportion of suicides using firearms), and negatively with the strictness of gun control laws and urbanization. Controls for other variables eliminated some of these associations, but firearm prevalence remained significant. In the Pearson correlations, all aspects of gun control were negatively associated with the firearm suicide rate (crime deterrence laws, government control laws, possession laws, safety laws, and sales restriction laws). Price, et al. did not study the non-firearm suicide rate or the overall suicide rate.

## Youth Suicide Rates

Webster, et al. (2004) studied the effect of state and federal laws relevant to youth firearm ownership (such as a minimum age for purchasing a firearm and safe-storage laws). Safe storage laws were associated with a lower suicide rate in youths aged 14-17, as well as a lower firearm suicide rate (but there was no association with the non-firearm suicide rate). For youths aged 18-20, all three suicide rates were lower in states with safe storage laws. A minimum age for purchasing and possession of a firearm did not have a significant impact on youth suicide rates.

Gius (2015) used panel data (50 states and 30 years) and found that the federal minimum age law (banning possession of handguns by those under the age of 18) passed in 1994 had a significant impact on the youth suicide rate, which dropped by 1.2% after the passage of the law. State minimum age laws did not have any additional impact. State child access prevention laws (which vary from state to state) also had a preventive impact on youth suicide rates.

## Studies in Other Countries

### Australia

Cantor and Lewin (1990) noted that Queensland, Australia, had weaker gun control laws than other states. From 1961-1985, Queensland had a higher suicide rate, a higher suicide rate using firearms and a greater proportion of suicides using firearms. Snowdon and Harris (1992) noted that South Australia restricted firearms in 1980. The male firearm suicide rate declined after this, but there was an increase in the male suicide rate by other methods. In other Australian states, however, both the firearm and non-firearm suicide rates rose from prior to 1980 to after 1980. In 1992, a stricter gun control law took effect in Queensland. Cantor and Slater (1995) found that the number of firearm suicides dropped afterwards by 21%, primarily in men, in urban areas and for 15-29-year-olds. Although the use of drugs and hanging for suicide increased in urban areas, the total number of suicides decreased. (In rural areas, the use of methods other than firearms did not change).

Australia passed a law in 1996 to control access and storage of firearms. Klieve, et al. (2009) found that the law was followed by a decreasing rate of firearm suicide (a trend that had begun prior to passage of the law), and an increase in the hanging suicide rate, resulting in no change in the overall suicide rate.

### Austria

Austria passed stricter gun control laws in 1997, raising the minimum age for purchase to 21 and instituting checks on safe storage. Niederkrotenthaler, et al. (2009) found that, after a temporary increase in the youth suicide rate in 1998, there was a continual decrease thereafter. The authors suggested that brief temporary increase was perhaps a result of the media coverage of firearms accompanying the legal change. Kapusta, et al. (2007) found a decrease in the firearm suicide rate after the 1997 change in laws, and this was found for all sex-by-age groups except women over the age of 64 and youths under that age of 20.

## Canada

Mundt (1990) found that tightening the gun control law in Canada in 1977 was associated with a lowering of the firearm suicide rate, even though the overall suicide rate and firearm ownership increased. Carrington and Moyer (1994a, 1994b) also found that the firearm suicide rate declined after passage of the law, but not the suicide rate by all other methods. Thus, displacement to other methods did not appear to occur. These trends were found in the provinces as well as the whole of Canada. Rich, et al. (1990) documented that the imposition of strict gun control laws in Toronto resulted in a decrease in the use of guns for suicide and a corresponding increase in the use of jumping (primarily in front of subway trains). Thus, apparently, people switched methods for suicide.

Sloan, et al. (1990) compared suicide in Seattle (USA) and Vancouver (Canada) in 1985-1987, regions which presumably differ in gun ownership and gun control laws. The suicide rates were similar, but the handgun suicide rate was higher in Seattle. In contrast, the suicide rates using poisoning, hanging and jumping/drowning were higher in Vancouver. Thus, there appeared to be evidence for switching methods when guns were less available. However, for those aged 15-24, the suicide rate was higher in Seattle and attributable to guns. Thus, Sloan concluded that gun control might lower the suicide rate in young adults.

Carrington (1999) examined the impact of firearm control law Bill C-51 in 1977 in Canada. Carrington's analysis (looking at changes in the slopes of the linear trends in rates before and after passage of the bill) found a decrease in the firearm suicide rate after passage of the bill, but no increase in the suicide rate by all other methods. Similar results were found for homicide.

Bridges (2004) compared suicide and homicide in Canada before and after the passage of Bill C-17 in 1991 which imposed restrictions on firearms. The firearm suicide rate declined after passage of the bill, but the overall suicide rate did not change significantly. For homicide, the rate of homicide by firearms and by all other methods both declined after passage of the bill.

### New Zealand

New Zealand toughened firearm laws in 1992, requiring licenses to own a gun, passing a test on basic regulations for gun ownership, and police approval of gun purchases. After the passage of the law, the firearm suicide rate dropped by 46%. (66% for youth aged 15-24 and 39% for adults). The proportion of suicides using firearms also dropped, but there was no change in the overall suicide rate (Beautrais, et al, 2006).

## GUN OWNERSHIP

### Household Gun Ownership

Clarke and Jones (1989) noted that the suicide rate in the United States increased from 1959 to 1984, primarily because of those using firearms for suicide. During the same period, household ownership of handguns (but not rifles and shot guns) increased. Clarke and Jones showed that ownership of handguns was associated over time with the firearm suicide rate, but not with the total suicide rate. Thus, Clarke and Jones could not determine whether the suicide rate increased because there were more handguns available or whether people who would have used other methods for suicide had switched to using handguns.

Boor (1981) found that, from 1962-1975 in the United States, as domestic production and importing of firearms increased, so did the firearm suicide rate. Wintemute (1988) found that the number of domestically produced handguns each year from 1946 to 1985 was positively associated with the firearm suicide rate.

Birckmayer and Hemenway (2001) examined panel data (9 census divisions over 15 years) and found that gun ownership predicted the suicide rate for 15-24-year-olds and 65-84-year-olds. Gun ownership predicted the firearm suicide rate for those aged 15-24, 45-64 and 65-84, but not those aged 25-44. Firearm ownership did not predict the non-firearm suicide for any of the age groups.

Over the provinces of Canada, Carrington and Moyer (1994a) found that the firearm suicide rate (but not the suicide rate by all other methods) was associated with the percentage of households owning guns.

Ajdacic-Gross, et al. (2010) compared the household ownership of firearms in the cantons of Switzerland with the proportion of suicides by firearms. For both men and women, the association was positive and statistically significant. Reisch, et al. (2013) studied suicide in Switzerland after the Swiss government halved the size of the armed forces in 2003-2004, mainly by earlier discharge (from 43 to 33) and enlisting fewer recruits. In addition, retired soldiers had to pay a higher fee to purchase their military firearm. After this change, the overall suicide rate and the firearm suicide rate decreased in men aged 18-43, but there was no change in the non-firearm suicide rate, indicating an absence of switching. These changes were not found in the suicide rates of women, nor in men aged 44-53.

Killias (1993) found that estimates of the percentage of households with guns in twelve nations was positively associated with the suicide rate using firearms (the total suicide rate and the percentage of suicides using guns), but not with the suicide rate by all other methods. Killias, et al. (2001) obtained measures of household gun ownership for 21 countries in a year close to 1990. This measure was positively associated with the firearm suicide rate, both for men and women, and with the homicide firearm rate, but not with the total suicide or homicide rates.

Ajdacic-Gross, et al. (2006) obtained data on the suicide rate and proportion of suicides by firearms for the years 1983 and 2000 and proportion of households with guns in 1989 and 2000 for nine countries. (Other countries in the data set had incomplete data for these years.) In 8 of the 9 countries, household ownership of firearms declined from 1989 to 2000. (The exception was Switzerland.). Of the 8 countries with declining household firearm ownership, 7 experienced a decline in the proportion of suicides using firearms. The Netherlands was the exception (along with Switzerland). Seven of the countries experienced a decline in the overall suicide rate (with Australia and Scotland being the exception).

## Gun Dealers

Gundlach (1990) measured firearm availability in the SMSAs of America by counting retail outlets in the Yellow Pages. For the 77 largest SMSAs, the divorce rate predicted the suicide rate in regions with both high availability and low availability of firearms and for both male and female suicide rates. Living alone predicted the suicide rate only when firearm availability was high. For the nine major regions of the United States, the firearm suicide rate was strongly associated with the Yellow Pages measure of firearm availability (measured for only the largest SMSAs in each region) and with the percentages owning guns.

## Hunting Licenses

Siegel and Rothman (2016) used a proxy measure of gun ownership (per capita hunting licenses and percentage of suicides using firearms) for the American states for the period 1981-2013 (panel data). For men, the higher the gun ownership, the higher the overall suicide rate and the firearm suicide rate and the lower the non-firearm suicide rate. For women, the higher the gun ownership, the higher the firearm suicide and the lower the non-firearm suicide rate, and there was no association with the overall suicide rate, and so there was evidence of switching methods for the women.

Simon, et al. (1996) found that the firearms suicide rate in the regions of Quebec (Canada) was associated with the density of hunting licenses (and with the total suicide rate).

### The Accidental Firearm Death Rate

In a time-series study, Bridges (2002) used the accidental firearm death rate in 1970-1998 in Canada as a measure of gun ownership and found that this annual measure was positively associated with the annual percentage suicides using firearms and the annual percentage of victims murdered with firearms. The association between the accidental firearm death rate and the percentage of suicides using firearms was found for all age groups except those over the age of 55.

Bridges and Kunselman (2004) examined the association between the accidental firearm death rate and the percentage of suicides-plus-homicides using firearms in Canada for the period 1974-1999. These measures were positively associated with the firearm suicide rate, negatively associated with the suicide rate by all other methods, and not significantly associated with the overall suicide rate. The associations for homicide were more supportive of non-switching of methods, although all three homicide rates (overall, firearm homicide rate and homicide rate by all other methods) were all positively associated with the measures of firearm availability.

## Guns in the Home

### Who Owns Guns?

Smith, et al. (2015) studied veterans in residential PTSD treatment and found that 32% owned a gun. Those with current suicidal ideation and prior suicide attempts were less likely to own a gun. More frequent combat exposure (but not the severity of PTSD symptoms) was positively associated with gun ownership. Depending on the source of the sample (VA versus a not-for-profit center) and suicidality, 61% to 75% said that they currently followed safe storage practices.

Freeman, et al. (1994) found that all of their sample of combat veterans with post-traumatic stress disorder had owned guns and three-quarters still did. Over half had loaded a gun at some point in order to die by suicide, and a third had done this while intoxicated.

## Gun Ownership by Suicides

Kellermann, et al. (1992) found that those dying by suicide at home were more likely to have a gun in the home, not graduate from high school, live alone, have been hospitalized for drinking, be on medication, use illicit drugs, and have had more quarrels/fights, arrests, and depression/mental illness than living controls from the same communities. The presence of a gun was significant in the multiple regression. The risk of suicide at home was even higher when the gun was handgun, loaded and kept in unlocked storage.

Brent, et al. (1993b) found that adolescent suicides with no psychiatric diagnosis more often had a loaded gun in the home than adolescent suicides with a psychiatric disorder. Brent, et al. (1993a) found that adolescent suicides who used a firearm for their suicide more often had a gun in the home, completed suicide in the home, were intoxicated with alcohol at the time, and were white and of lower social class. They did not differ in psychiatric diagnosis or life stressors. The more handguns in the home, the higher the percentage of the suicides using a firearm for the suicide, an association that was found in urban areas only and which was stronger in the non-disturbed suicides, but which remained significant after controls for psychiatric disturbance and prior suicide attempts. The suicides, in general, more often had access to handguns (but not long guns) in the home than community controls.

Shah, et al. (2000) compared 36 adolescent suicides in Colorado with age and sex matched controls selected from the same schools. Twenty-four of the suicides used a firearm. The firearm suicides were more likely to have a gun in the home than the controls (72% vs 50%), and the suicides were also more likely to be in home with an unlocked gun and homes with more than one gun.

Bailey, et al. (1997) found that female suicides in three counties in America (in KY, OH and WA) more often had a gun in the home than did neighbors (as well as more often living alone and having a history of mental illness).

Cummings, et al. (1997) found that suicides (and homicide victims) in Washington state during the period 1980-1992 were more likely to have a handgun in the home purchased by themselves from a licensed dealer than living matched controls.[7] The effect persisted for up to five years after the purchase, was found for all calibers (.22 to .30 and .32 to .45), and was stronger the more handgun purchases made. The effect was not affected by sex, age or neighborhood (classified by median family income).

Houtsma and Anestis (2017) studied individuals who had made a suicide attempt in the past. Their estimate of the likelihood of a future suicide attempt was not associated with handgun ownership in the total sample. However, the association between current suicidal ideation and their estimate of a future suicide attempt was stronger in those who owned a handgun than in those who did not. Houtsma and Anestis argued, therefore, that ownership of a handgun might facilitate the transition from suicidal ideation to suicide attempt.

Hintikka, et al. (1997) studied 68 suicides aged 15-24 in one part of Finland, of whom 62% used firearms for their suicide; 74% of these firearm suicides used licensed hunting guns (owned by someone), with 31% owned legally by the suicide. Shotguns were the most common type of gun used (60% of all firearm suicides). Hintikka, et al. argued that the availability of hunting guns accounted for the very high rate of youth suicide in this region (51 per 100,000 per year).

---

[7] The effect was present for purchases by another family member, but not statistically significant.

Beautrais, et al. (1996) compared completed suicides, medically serious attempted suicides and healthy controls in New Zealand. Firearms were used by 13.3% of the suicides and 1.3% of the serious suicide attempts. Those using firearms for a suicidal action had an 83.3% risk of dying. Overall, 92% of those using a firearm for suicide or attempted suicide had a firearm in the home, compared to 10% of those who used other methods. However, firearms were not more common in the homes of completed and attempted suicides than in the homes of the control subjects, even after adjusting for recent psychiatric problems.

## Firearm Storage

Brent, et al. (1991) compared adolescent completed suicides, attempted suicides and psychiatric controls. Sixty-nine percent of the completers used guns for the suicidal act versus none of the attempters. More of the completers had guns available in the homes, and they had more total guns and more handguns available. They did not differ in the method of storage of guns or whether the gun was stored loaded.

Caron (2004; Caron, et al. 2008) examined the impact of a law in Canada passed in 1992 requiring safe storage of firearms on the suicide rate in northern Quebec in the six years prior to and after the passage of the law. The overall suicide rate rose in this region after the passage of the law, as did the suicide rate in all Quebec. The firearm suicide rate decreased after passage of the law, an effect found in men under the age of 45 and in women, but the suicide rate by all other methods increased. In particular, suicide rates by hanging rose after passage of the law. In Caron's second paper, he noted that these trends were not statistically significant and were a continuation of trends apparent before passage of the law.

Kposowa, et al. (2016) studied the household ownership of firearms in the states of America, whether they were loaded, and whether they were stored unlocked. They found that all three of these measures, along with the strictness of the state firearm control laws, predicted the state suicide rates and the state firearm suicide rates. However, Kposowa et al. did not study the impact of these variables on the non-firearm suicide rates.

Watkins and Lizotte (2011) used data from a national survey of middle and high school students to identify roughly 575 adolescents who had attempted suicide in the previous year. Those who had attempted suicide were more likely to report a handgun in the home (21.3% vs 13.1%), even after controlling for other factors, but not a long gun (7.7% vs 8.6%). More complex analyses (many of the adolescents were interviewed twice and changes in home ownership of guns and suicide attempt status could be examined) did not confirm the relevance of home ownership of guns on suicide attempts, but the sample sizes were small for these analyses.

Grossman, et al. (2005) examined youths who used firearms to attempt or complete suicide or who unintentionally injured others ("case" youths) with control households with children and firearms at home. The cases were more like to have a firearm owned by the youth, had firearms more often purchased for protection and less often for hunting, more likely to have owned the firearms for less than five years, less likely to have their guns stored unloaded, stored locked and stored separately from the ammunition, or to have the ammunition locked. Locking the firearm in a safe was more important than having a trigger lock or an on-gun device. Safe storage appeared to be useful for both handguns and long guns.

Khazem, et al. (2016) studied military personnel who owned firearms. Roughly 4% reported a prior suicide attempt, and 8.2% current suicidal ideation. About 18% reported keeping their firearms loaded and unsecured. Firearm storage was not associated with current suicidal ideation. However, the association between current suicidal ideation and their estimate likelihood of a suicide attempt was moderated by storing their firearms loaded and unsecured. For those storing their firearms loaded and unsecured, the association was greater, and these individuals also reported less fear about death.

### Israeli Policies for Armed Forces

In 2006, Israel ordered soldiers visiting their homes on weekends to leave their firearms on the base. The suicide rate in this group (soldiers aged 18-21) of the population dropped by 40%, primarily a result of the lower firearm suicide rate on weekends (Lubin, et al., 2010).

### Gun Ownership in Finland

Lahti, et al. (2014) noted that gun ownership was higher in the north of Finland than in the south (50 versus 27 per 100 persons). Comparing the suicide rates of those under the age of 45, the firearms suicide rate was higher in the north (221 vs. 104 per 100,000 per year). The suicide rates by all other methods did not differ. The same difference was found in the percentage of suicides using firearms, and those in the north used both handguns and long guns more often for their suicides.

## The Role of Alcohol

Branas, et al. (2011) studied a sample of suicides in Philadelphia and control residents. They found that excessive alcohol intake was positively associated with firearm suicide. However, the availability of local alcohol outlets (on-site and off-site) was not associated with firearm suicide. Incidentally, 31% of the firearm suicides had imbibed alcohol, 19.9% excessively.

## Who Uses Guns for Suicide?

Restricting access to and ownership of firearms will have a major impact only if guns are used frequently for suicide. Lester (1990) provided the suicide rate by guns and by all other methods for 20 countries in 1980 (see Table 1).

**Table 1. Suicide rates by method, 1980**

| Country | Suicide rate per 100,000 per year | | |
|---|---|---|---|
| | by gun | by all other methods | percentage by gun |
| Australia | 3.52 | 7.42 | 32% |
| Austria | 3.13 | 22.47 | 12% |
| Belgium | 2.62 | 19.42 | 12% |
| Canada | 4.66 | 9.30 | 33% |
| Denmark | 2.36 | 29.21 | 7% |
| Finland | 6.74 | 18.91 | 26% |
| France | 4.16 | 15.22 | 21% |
| Hungary | 0.63 | 44.27 | 1% |
| Israel | 1.68 | 4.28 | 28% |
| Italy | 0.96 | 6.40 | 13% |
| Japan | 0.08 | 17.47 | 0.5% |
| Netherlands | 0.22 | 10.79 | 2% |
| New Zealand | 2.12 | 8.71 | 20% |
| Norway | 3.06 | 9.34 | 25% |
| Scotland | 0.52 | 9.47 | 5% |
| Sweden | 2.29 | 17.09 | 12% |
| US | 6.76 | 5.04 | 56% |
| Venezuela | 1.04 | 3.76 | 22% |
| West Germany | 1.30 | 19.60 | 6% |
| Yugoslavia | 0.93 | 13.77 | 6% |

It can be see than the USA had the highest percentage use of firearms for suicide (56%) followed by Canada (33%) and Australia (32%). In contrast, firearms were used rarely for suicide in Hungary (1%) and Japan (0.5%). Restricting access to firearms would, therefore, have more of potential impact on suicide in the USA, Canada and Australia than in other countries.

Lester used the percentage of homicides committed using a firearm as a measure of the availability of firearms, and this percentage was positively associated with the suicide rate by guns and negatively with the suicide rate by all other methods (Pearson correlations 0.38 and -0.55, respectively). The percentage of homicides by gun and the percentage of suicides by gun were positively associated (r = - 0.64).

Firearms are used more for suicide by men than by women. Stack (2015a) provided data on this for a recent year (in the 2000s) using WHO data (see Table 2). It can be seen that, in all countries, firearms were used more often for suicide by men than by women. In addition, it should be noted that, in all of the countries listed in Table 2, males have a higher suicide rate than do females. Restricting access to firearms would, therefore, have more of potential impact on suicide in men than on suicide in women.

Stack noted that suicide by gun was the second most prevalent method for suicide in men in these nations. A suicide attempt using guns is one the most lethal methods for suicide, with approximately 95% of attempts proving to be fatal. Stack found that the percentage of suicides using guns was unrelated to the male suicide rate, with guns playing a minor role in many nations with very high male suicide rates (Estonia [41.4], Latvia [50.6], Lithuania [75.1] and Slovenia [38.1]). In contrast, the USA, 61% of the male suicides used firearms, but the male suicide rate was only 15.9.

Tewksbury, et al. (2010) compared men who used firearms and hanging for suicide in Louisville (Kentucky). The use of a firearm was more common in older men, if they had drugs in their system, if there was alcohol in their system and if they had a higher Body-Mass-Index. The two groups did not differ in leaving a suicide note.

Hempstead, et al. (2013) studied a large sample of male suicides in New Jersey (n = 3,413), of whom 33% used a firearm. Firearms were used for suicide more often by those over the age of 65 and by white and black suicides (as compared to Hispanic and Asian suicides). The firearm suicides were less likely to have psychiatric problems (current or past), but no less likely to be depressed. They were less likely to be substance abusers but more likely to have a physical health problem (especially cardiovascular, respiratory and cancer). Hempstead et al. hypothesized that gun ownership was associated with hyper-masculinity in men, and hyper-masculinity may be associated with neglect of physical health and poor tolerance for disabilities and physical maladies.

**Table 2. Percentage of suicides by firearm**

| Country | Men | Women |
|---|---|---|
| Argentina | 37.6 | 25.9 |
| Australia | 11.5 | 2.6 |
| Austria | 20.7 | 2.6 |
| Brazil | 22.1 | 13.4 |
| Canada | 21.6 | 3.8 |
| Chile | 11.7 | 8.0 |
| Colombia | 38.0 | 15.0 |
| Costa Rica | 24.0 | 11.3 |
| Croatia | 25.4 | 4.5 |
| Cuba | 3.4 | 0.7 |
| Czech Republic | 12.4 | 2.6 |
| Denmark | 14.5 | 0.8 |
| Dominican Republic | 20.2 | 8.4 |
| Ecuador | 19.2 | 5.3 |
| El Salvador | 3.8 | 1.4 |
| Estonia | 9.1 | 1.3 |
| Finland | 26.7 | 2.6 |
| France | 22.1 | 4.1 |
| Georgia | 3.2 | 0.8 |
| Germany | 10.3 | 1.4 |
| Hong Kong | 0.3 | 0.1 |
| Hungary | 4.0 | 0.6 |
| Iceland | 19.5 | 0.0 |
| Israel | 25.4 | 9.1 |
| Japan | 0.2 | 0.0 |
| Kuwait | 0.5 | 0.0 |
| Latvia | 6.5 | 0.9 |
| Lithuania | 2.7 | 0.3 |
| Luxembourg | 14.6 | 3.2 |
| Malta | 15.8 | 0.0 |
| Mexico | 20.5 | 13.4 |
| Moldova | 2.4 | 0.5 |
| Netherlands | 4.4 | 0.6 |
| New Zealand | 11.2 | 2.2 |
| Nicaragua | 7.4 | 1.7 |
| Norway | 27.1 | 2.0 |

| Country | Men | Women |
|---|---|---|
| Panama | 11.9 | 2.2 |
| Paraguay | 30.4 | 21.5 |
| Peru | 11.8 | 1.2 |
| Poland | 1.1 | 0.2 |
| Portugal | 11.1 | 3.2 |
| Puerto Rico | 17.6 | 6.9 |
| Romania | 1.0 | 0.1 |
| Serbia | 20.1 | 5.2 |
| Slovakia | 12.3 | 2.9 |
| Slovenia | 11.8 | 1.2 |
| South Africa | 12.6 | 9.2 |
| South Korea | 0.4 | 0.1 |
| Spain | 7.1 | 0.9 |
| Sweden | 17.1 | 0.9 |
| Switzerland | 33.5 | 3.4 |
| Thailand | 6.1 | 1.9 |
| United Kingdom | 3.5 | 0.6 |
| Uruguay | 47.8 | 35.7 |
| US | 60.6 | 35.7 |
| Venezuela | 23.3 | 12.2 |

Kaplan, et al. (2012) studied 4,338 men over the age of 65 who died by suicide in the United States, some 80% of whom used firearms. Those using firearms were more often rural dwelling, white and veterans, less often lived in the north-east of the United States, but did not differ in marital status. Those using firearms more often had physical health problems, less often had financial or legal problems, and less often had psychiatric problems and a history of suicidality. However, they did not differ in current depression, substance abuse or disclosing their intent to die.

In a study of both adult men and women who died by suicide, Kaplan, et al. (2009) found that firearms were used more by men than by women (58% vs. 31%). For the men, using a firearm was positively associated with firearm availability, raised blood alcohol concentration, acute crisis and relationship problems and negatively associated with diagnosis of a mental health problem, a history of suicide attempts or alcohol problems. For the women, using a firearm was positively associated with being older, married, white and a veteran, residing in areas with higher rates of firearm availability, having an acute crisis, having experienced the death of a relative or friend, being depressed, and having relationship problems and negatively associated with a treated DSM-IV-diagnosed problem, previous suicide attempts and physical health problems.

Anestis (2016) studied a large sample of suicides in the United States and compared those who used firearms with those who used other methods. He found that only 12% of the suicides by firearms had made previous suicide attempts as compared to 29% of those using other methods. This may result from the greater lethality of firearms as a method for suicide (so that they are more likely to die as a result of their first attempt), and to the impulsive nature of firearm suicides. Anestis, et al. (2017) studied a small sample of 267 suicides and found that those who used guns were more often male and more often owned guns, but less often discussed suicide or made a previous suicide attempt. Anestis, et al. (2017), in this same sample of 267 suicides, also compared those who owned guns with those who did not own guns. Gun ownership was associated with being male, being married, being a veteran and being heterosexual, having children, living in the Southern states, and not having made a previous suicide attempt.

Hoffmire and Bossarte (2014) looked at suicides from nine states and found that military veteran status affected choice of method for suicide. Males veterans were 6% more likely to use a firearm for their suicide and female veterans 18% more likely compared to non-veteran peers. McCarten, et al. (2015) found that 69% of male veterans and 40% of female veterans used firearms for their suicides in the 2000s. From 2000 to 2010, the firearm suicide rate of veterans rose 16.2% for male veterans and 75.4% for female veterans. However, the non-firearm suicide rate also rose for both men and women (12.5% and 12.8%, respectively), resulting in an increase in the total suicide rate (14.7% and 34.6% for men and women, respectively).

In Queensland (Australia), Tait and Carpenter (2009) found that firearms were used for suicide most by elderly men and those in rural areas and less often by Aborigines. Firearms suicides were less likely to have psychiatric problems and prior suicidal behavior.

Marks and Stokes (1976) surveyed students in Georgia and Wisconsin about their experience with firearms (had they ever fired a gun, were there guns in their home, etc.). They found that men had more experience with firearms than women, and Georgia students more than Wisconsin students. Marks and Stokes, argued, therefore, that choice of a weapon for suicide might depend on the individual's experience with guns, with men and Southerners more experienced with firearms and, therefore, more likely to choose a firearm for suicide.

Sarma and Kola (2010a, 2010b) compared 793 firearm suicides in Ireland with 8,881 non-firearm suicides. The firearm suicides were more often male, living in rural areas, farm employed and aged 20-25.

## Regional Differences

Nestadt, et al. (2017) examined suicides in Maryland (US) and found that the firearm suicide rate was higher in rural areas than in urban areas, whereas the non-firearm suicide rate was similar in rural and urban areas. Most (89%) of the firearm suicides were by men, and the higher firearm suicide rate in rural areas was found only in men.

Brown, et al. (2014) compared the American states with a culture of honor (historically with Scottish and Irish immigrants and known for their high rates of interpersonal violence) in the south and southwest, with the remaining states and found that white (but not non-white) firearm suicide rates were higher in the culture of honor states, even after controlling for temperature, gun ownership and other possible confounding variables. For whites, culture of honor and gun ownership predicted firearm suicide rates while, for non-whites, only gun ownership predicted firearm suicide rates. The temperature, economic deprivation and access to health care did not predict firearm suicide rates for either group.

## What Type of Gun Is Used?

There are, of course, many types of guns. In 2017 and 2018, the USA witnessed several mass shootings by individuals armed with AK-47 firearms, and there were calls to ban or restrict these weapons. However, from the point of view of suicide prevention, suicidal individuals do not kill themselves with AK 47s. Banning assault weapons may be a good idea, but it will have little impact on suicide.

Browning (1974) studied a small sample of 82 suicides in Cuyahoga County (Ohio), of whom 35 used firearms (83% of these used handguns). Only three (all handguns) of these were obtained specifically for the purpose of suicide. Fifteen were obtained for protection (but had never been used for this purpose), five for hunting and three for the person's job. (The reasons for nine were unknown). Four of the firearms used for suicide were owned by family members and four by non-family members (three friends and one landlord).

Zwerling, et al. (1993) studied firearm suicides in Iowa in 1980-1984 and 1990-1991. The use of handguns for suicide become more common from the first to the second period, and the use of rifles less common. (The use of shotguns remained consistent.) For the period 1990-1991, 41% of the male suicides used handguns, 42% shotguns and 17% rifles. For the female suicides, 85% used handguns, 10% shotguns and 5% rifles. Although the use of handguns overall for suicide rose from 1980-1984 to 1990-1991 from 37% to 44%, estimates of household ownership of handguns did not change (16.5% to 16.3%). Clearly, handguns were used more for suicide than their prevalence in the state.

Frei, et al. (2006) studied a sample of 447 suicides in Basle, Switzerland, where military service is common and where many citizens possess firearms. Of the 134 firearm suicides, 81 used a private weapon and 53 an army weapon. For the private weapons, four were rifles and 68 military handguns (with 10 unknown). Of the army weapons, 6 were rifles, 21 pistols, and 23 semi-automatic weapons (and one unknown). In one case, the pistol of a customs officer was used. A firearm was used more often by men, and those using army firearms were younger than those using private firearms and other methods for suicide. Those using army firearms were younger, more often single, less often had a psychiatric problem and less often a history of suicide attempts.

In 1980, a small proportion of death certificates of those who used firearms to die by suicide were coded for the type of firearms used (n = 15,412). Of these, 13.7% used a handgun, 12.8% used a shotgun and 6.6% used a rifle, with 66.8% "unknown." Lester and Frank (1988) studied these data and found that states with stricter handgun control laws had a lower percentage of suicides using handguns (Pearson $r = -0.37$, $p < .01$). Handguns were used relatively more often by women than by men (67.6% versus 37.1%), more often by nonwhites than by whites (50.4% versus 40.7%) and by those aged more than 25 than by younger suicides (44.2% versus 31.5%). Single individuals used handguns relatively less often than those with other marital statuses (34.2% versus 50.2%).

Time (July 17, 1989) published a listing of all firearms deaths in the USA for the first seven day of May. 1989. Lester (1989) analyzed these data and reported that, of the 184 of the 216 suicides for whom the type of gun was noted, 63% used handguns. For the 100 murders for which the type of gun was noted (out of 211 homicides), 77% were handguns. Of the 15 accidental deaths for which the type of gun was noted (out of 25), 67% were from handguns. Lester found that difference between suicides and homicides was statistically significant. Lester also compared those using handguns versus long guns and found no difference by sex or age. For those with data available, 75% of the men and 71% of the women who died by suicide shot themselves in the head. Women did not, therefore, appear to avoid facial disfigurement as has been suggested by Lester (1988b).

Incidentally, regarding murder, Linsky, et al. (1995) calculated the murder rate by handguns and by long guns for each state in America. For 1980-1984. Lester (1998a) found that the percentage of murders committed with long guns (but not the murder rate using long guns) was higher in states which were more rural and in which more hunting licenses per capita were issued.

Wright, et al. (2008) examined 336 firearm suicides in California by those under the age of 21. They found that 65% of the suicides occurred at the suicide's residence and 10% at the home of family members or friends; 63% used a handgun and 31% a long gun; 19% were owned by the suicide, 31% by a household member (most often a family member), 15% by someone else and 45% unspecified.

Choi, et al. (2017) studied 3,116 youth suicides under the age of 21 in the United States for the period 2005-2014, comparing those who used firearms with those who used other methods for suicide. Firearm suicides were less likely to have been identified as having mental problems and, for males, less likely to have a history of attempted suicide or suicidal intent. The use of firearms was less common in the northeastern states, more often used by males, the older youths, and those on active military duty. The significant predictors of firearms use were sex (male), age (older), ethnicity (white), region (not Northeast), prior attempted suicide (no) and mental health problems (no). Where ownership was noted (for only roughly one-third of the suicides), 65% of the youths used firearms owned by parents or other family members. Only 23% used a firearm that they owned. Handguns were used by 55%, rifles 19% and shotguns 18%.

Sanaei-Zadeh, et al. (2004) examined 27 firearm suicides in Iran. All were young males, and 26 of them used military rifles. Twenty-two (82%) had one entrance wound, with the remainder having multiple entrance wounds. The location of the wound was 37% submentum (under the chin [the fascial space of the head and neck]), 26% chest, 25% center of the face and 11% forehead. Twenty-three were contact or near-contact wounds. Almost all (96%) occurred at garrisons or police stations. This type of study would be extremely valuable for large samples of suicides in the United States (and other countries).

## Discussion

This is an area in which much more research should be carried out. In the limited data available, handguns and rifles were used most often for suicide, with shotguns less often used. Firearms were used by suicidal individuals in some locations more than others, and by some types of people more than others (for example, by men). The ideal research would involve investigating each suicide firearm and ascertaining:

1. Which type of gun was used?
2. Where the bullet entered the body?
3. Who owned the gun?
4. When was it purchased?
5. How was it stored by the suicide/owner?
6. What other guns did the suicide/owner own?

The answers to these questions might provide some guidance for suicide prevention.

## THE LOCATION OF FIREARM SUICIDES

About 75.4% of suicides in the US occur in the home (Stack, 2015b). The next most common locales are natural areas (4.1%), streets/highways (3.2%), motor vehicles (2.3%) and hotels/motels (1.9%). Those choosing natural areas for their suicides are less likely to use a firearm (42.7% vs 51.2%) and more likely to use drowning, fall/jump, and poisons (Stack, 2015c), and this was especially true for suicides choosing the Grand Canyon National Park, where 15.0% used firearms compared to 42.7% in other natural areas (Stack & Bowman, 2015).

Stack (2015d) focused on one particular pattern which he named the *Paladin Pattern*, after the television show *Have Gun, Will Travel*, in which Richard Boone played a character called Paladin. In a data set based on select states in 2003-2006 from the USA, Stack identified 3,437 suicides by firearm away from home. Compared to 27,133 other suicides, the Paladin Pattern suicides were more often male (90.3% vs 76.9%), less often with a previous suicide attempt (8.7% vs 18.6%) and in current treatment for mental health (17.7% vs 29.4%), and more often in trouble with the criminal justice system (14.0% vs 8.7%) and a violence perpetrator (8.6% vs 4.3%). In a regression analysis, the Paladin Pattern was found more in men, Caucasians. married (vs single) and younger individuals. Drug and alcohol use lessened the likelihood of the Paladin Pattern with the exception of marihuana which increased the likelihood. Paladin Pattern suicides were more likely to leave a suicide note.[8]

## The Mental Health of Gun Owners

Sorenson and Vittes (2008) analyzed data from the General Social Survey and found no difference in the general and emotional mental health, mental health help seeking, functional mental health (e.g., problems at work) or sadness and depression of gun owners, those who lived in a house with a gun owner and those with no access to guns in the home. Thus, the high risk of suicide in those living in homes with guns does not appear to be related to differences in mental health.

Miller, et al. (2009) analyzed data from the National Comorbidity Survey Replication in the United States. In this sample, one third (35%) of the respondents lived in homes with a firearm present. Comparing those living in homes with firearms and those living in homes with no firearms, there were no differences in the two groups in the incidence of psychiatric disorder (anxiety disorders, mood disorders, or substance abuse) or in suicidal ideation and planning in the prior year. However, those living in home with a firearm were less likely to have made a serious suicide attempt in the past year (0.0% versus 0.7%).

[8] Clearly, some unusual suicides involve the use of a firearm, including Russian roulette, suicide-by-cop, and some in public (such as on live television). For such cases, see Lester and Stack (2015).

# Evaluating Prevention Tactics

## Safety Training by Professionals

One tactic for reducing unsafe storage and other dangerous practices is to have physicians and counsellors talk to their patients and clients about these practices. Slovak and Brewer (2010) surveyed social workers on their attitudes toward this tactic. They found that the attitude was more positive if they had received training in this tactic and were from urban areas, and there was a trend for male social workers, social workers with a higher proportion of male clients, and LISWs (Licensed Independent Social Workers) to have a more positive attitude toward this tactic.

Kaplan, et al. (1998) gave a questionnaire to a sample of primary care physicians and found that only 58% asked depressed older patients (or their families) whether they had access to a firearm. Those who asked were more likely to be specialists in geriatrics and to have confidence in their ability to assess and treat depression and suicidality, more often in rural areas and with a higher proportion of older patients. They were also more likely to use mental health assessment tools, and they were more likely to have had continuing training in suicide risk assessment.

## Working with Gun Dealers

Vriniotis, et al. (2015) developed materials for firearm dealers on selling guns to suicidal people (tip sheets, DVDs and check-lists) and for their customers on gun safety practices (posters, brochures and wallet cards). Six months after distributing the materials, the gun dealers were visited, and 48% had at least some materials on display. The gun dealers were more positive about the materials for customers than for the materials for themselves.

## Working with High-Risk Psychiatric Patients

Vars, et al. (2017) explored whether psychiatric patients (in-patient and out-patient) would be willing to have their names placed on a do-not-sell list if such a list were available. There were two options: a notarized form to get on the list followed by (1) a notarized form and a 7-day delay period to get off the list or (2) the procedure in (1) plus a judicial hearing to have their name removed from the list. Of those surveyed 40% said that they would agree to proposal (1) and 36% for proposal (2). Most of the demographic and personal characteristics were not associated with agreeing to either proposal (e.g., sex, race, psychiatric diagnosis), but older patients were more willing to sign up while those with access to a gun were less willing to sign up.

## Educational Programs

Stanley, et al. (2017) compared educational videos on means safety versus means restriction. In a sample of undergraduates, a clinical vignette was presented involved a suicidal patient who owned a gun. The counselor in the vignette proposed talking about *means safety* or *means restriction*. Participants found the means safety version more acceptable: for example, more likely to tell their counselor that they owned a gun and more likely to limit their access to it. Scores were not associated with membership in the NRA or other gun organizations, approval of the Second Amendment, or lifetime suicidality.

Pope, et al. (2016) evaluated training gatekeepers (older adult caseworkers providing direct social service care) about suicide risk assessment and counseling about access to lethal means. In both areas, the gatekeepers improved in their knowledge, but their reluctance to engage in either activity remained unchanged.

## Discussion

These evaluations of programs are excellent, and more research of this kinds needs to be conducted.

# Conclusion

This body of research in impressive. There seems to be no doubt that firearms play a large role in suicide, and that appropriate gun control laws and regulations play a role in reducing the suicide rate. Three points are worth stressing.

First, the research reviewed here clearly supports the role of firearm availability in firearms being used for suicide. Legal restrictions, firearm ownership, and storage practices all contribute to the use of firearms for suicide, positively or negatively. However, as in Chapter 1, the evidence on whether switching methods for suicide occurs when firearms are less available is inconsistent. Some studies report no switching, some studies report switching, and some studies find that this conclusion depends on factors such as sex, age and other personal variables. As noted in Chapter 1, even if some people would switch methods for suicide if firearms were less available, they typically would have to switch to less lethal methods, making survival and intervention possible.

Second, the small study from Iran (Sanaei-Zadeh, et al., 2004) on the details of the firearm suicide gun shots needs to be replicated on large samples in the United States and other countries. Information on the number of shots fired and the location of the wounds may provide important cues for suicide prevention.

Finally, the few evaluation studies of prevention programs are interesting, but many more programs should be tried and, just as importantly, evaluated.

# REFERENCES


Ajdacic-Gross, V., Killias, M., Hepp, U., Gadola, E., Bopp, M., Lauber, C., Schnyder, U., Gutzwiller, F., & Rössier, W. (2006). Changing times. *American Journal of Public Health*, 96, 1752-1755.

Ajdacic-Gross, V., Killias, M., Hepp, U., Haymoz, S., Bopp, M., Gutzwiller, F., & Rössier, W. (2010). Firearm suicides and the availability of firearms. *European Psychiatry*, 25, 432-434.

Andres, A. R., & Hempstead, K. (2011). Gun control and suicide. *Health Policy*, 101, 95-103.

Anestis, M. D. (2016). Prior suicide attempts are less common in suicide decedents who died by firearms relative to those who died by other means. *Journal of Affective Disorders*, 189.

Anestis, M. D., & Anestis, J. C. (2015). Suicide rates and state laws regulating access and exposure to handguns. *American Journal of Public Health*, 105, 2049-2058.

Anestis, M. D., Anestis, J. C., & Butterworth, S. E. (2017). Handgun legislation and changes in statewide overall suicide rates. *American Journal of Public Health*, 107, 579-581.

Anestis, M. D., & Capron, D. W. (2016). The associations between state veteran population rates, handgun legislation, and statewide suicide rates. *Journal of Psychiatric Research*, 74, 30-34.

Anestis, M. D., Khazem, L. R., & Anestis, J. C. (2017). Differentiating suicide decedents who died using firearms from those who died using other methods. *Psychiatry Research*, 252, 23-28.

Anestis, M. D., Khazem, L. R., Law, K. C., Houtsma, C., LeTard, R., Moberg, F., & Martin, R. (2015). The association between state laws regulating handgun ownership and statewide sui106-109. cide rates. *American Journal of Public Health*, 105, 2059-2067.

Bailey, J. E., Kellerman, A. L., Somes, G. W., Banton, J. G., Rivara, F. P., & Rushforth, N. P. (1997). Risk factors for violent death of women in the home. *Archives of Internal Medicine*, 157, 777-782.

Beautrais, A. L., Fergusson, D. M., & Horwood, L. J. (2006). Firearms legislation and reductions in firearm-related suicide deaths in New Zealand. *Australian & New Zealand Journal of Psychiatry*, 40, 253-259.

Beautrais, A. L., Joyce, P. R., & Mulder, R. T. (1996). Access to firearms and the risk of suicide. *Australian & New Zealand Journal of Psychiatry*, 30, 741-748.

Birckmayer, J., & Hemenway, D. (2001). Suicide and firearm prevalence. *Suicide & Life-Threatening Behavior*, 31, 303-310.

Boor, M. (1981). Methods of suicide and implications for suicide prevention. *Journal of Clinical Psychology*, 37, 70-75.

Boor, M., & Bair, J. H. (1990). Suicide rates, handgun control laws and sociodemographic variables. *Psychological Reports*, 66, 923-930.

Branas, C. C., Richmond, T. S., ten Have, T. R., & Wiebe, T. J. (2011). Acute alcohol consumption, alcohol outlets, and gun suicide. *Substance Use & Misuse*, 46, 1592-1603.

Brent, D. A., Perper, J. A., Allman, C. J., Moritz, G. M., Wartella, M. E., & Zelenak, J. P. (1991). The presence and accessibility of firearms in the homes of adolescent suicides. *Journal of the American Medical Association*, 266, 2989-2995.

Brent, D. A., Perper, J. A., Moritz, G. M., Baugher, M., & Allman, C. (1993b). Suicide in adolescents with no apparent psychopathology. *Journal of the American Academy of Child & Adolescent Psychiatry*, 32, 494-500.

Brent, D. A., Perper, J. A., Moritz, G. M., Baugher, M., Schweers, J., & Roth, C. (1993a). Firearms and adolescent suicide. *American Journal of Diseases of Children*, 147, 1066-1071.

Bridges, F. S. (2002). Gun availability and use of guns for murder and suicide in Canada. *Psychological Reports*, 90, 1257-1258.

Bridges, F. S. (2004). Gun control law (Bill C-17), suicide, and homicide in Canada. *Psychological Reports*, 94, 819-826.

Bridges, F. S., & Kunselman, J. C. (2004). Gun availability and use of guns for suicide, homicide, and murder in Canada. *Perceptual & Motor Skills,* 98, 594-598.

Brown, R. P., Imura, M., & Osterman, L. L. (2014). Gun culture. *Basic & Applied Social Psychology*, 36, 164-175.

Browning, C. H. (1974). Epidemiology of suicide. *Comprehensive Psychiatry*, 15, 549-553.

Cantor, C. H., & Slater, P. J. (1995). The impact of firearm control legislation on suicide in Queensland. *Medical Journal of Australia*, 162, 583-585.

Caron, J. (2004). Gun control and suicide. *Archives of Suicide Research*, 8, 361-374.

Caron, J., Julien, M., & Huang, J. H. (2008). Changes in suicide methods in Quebec between 1987 and 2000. *Suicide & Life-Threatening Behavior*, 38, 195-208.

Carrington, P. J. (1999). Gender, gun control, suicide and homicide in Canada. *Archives of Suicide Research,* 5, 71-75.

Carrington, P. J., & Moyer, S. (1994a). Gun availability and suicide in Canada. *Studies on Crime and Crime Prevention*, 3, 168-178.

Carrington, P. J., & Moyer, S. (1994b). Gun control and suicide in Ontario. *American Journal of Psychiatry,* 151, 606-608.

Chapman, S., Alpers, P., Agho, K., & Jones, M. (2006). Australia's 1996 gun law reforms. *Injury Prevention*, 12, 365-372.

Choi, N. G., DiNitto, D. M., & Marti, C. N. (2017). Youth firearm suicide. *Child & Youth Services Review,* 83, 9-16.

Clarke, R. V., & Jones, P. R. (1989). Suicide and increased availability of handguns in the United States. *Social Science & Medicine,* 28, 805-809.

Crifasi, C. K., Meyers, J. S., Vernick, J. S., & Webster, D. W. (2015). Effects of changes in permit-to-purchase handgun laws in Connecticut and Missouri on suicide rates. *Preventive Medicine*, 79, 43-49.

Cummings, P., Koepsell, T. D., Grossman, D. C., Savarino, J., & Thompson, R. S. (1997). The association between the purchase of a handgun and homicide and suicide. *American Journal of Public Health*, 87, 974-978.

Freeman, T., Clothier, J., Thornton, C., & Keesee, N. (1994). Firearm collection and use among combat veterans admitted to a posttraumatic stress disorder rehabilitation unit. *Journal of Nervous & Mental Disease,* 182, 592-594.

Frei, A., Han, A., Weiss, M. G., Dittmann, V., & Ajdacic-Gross, V. (2006). Use of army weapons and private firearms for suicide and homicide in the region of Basle, Switzerland. *Crisis,* 27, 140-146.

Gius, M. (2015). The impact of minimum age and child access prevention laws on firearm-related youth suicides and unintentional deaths. *The Social Science Journal*, 52, 168-175.

Grossman, D. C., Mueller, B. A., Riedy, C., Dowd, M. D., Villaveces, A., Prodzinski, J., Nakagawara, J., Howard, J., Thiersch, N., & Harruff, R. (2005). Gun storage practices and risk of youth suicide and unintentional firearm injuries. *Journal of the American Medical Association,* 293, 707-714.

Gundlach, J. H. (1990). Absence of family support, opportunity and suicide. *Family Perspectives,* 24(1), 7-13.

Hempstead, K., Nguyen, T., David-Rus, R., & Jacquemin, B. (2013). Health problems and male firearm suicide. *Suicide & Life-Threatening Behavior*, 43, 1-16.

Hintikka, J., Lehtonen, J., & Viinamäki, H. (1997). Hunting guns in homes and suicide in 15-24-year-old males in Eastern Finland. *Australian & New Zealand Journal of Psychiatry*, 31, 858-861.

IIoffmirc, C. A., & Bossarte, R. M. (2014). Λ reconsideration of the correlation between veteran status and firearm suicide in the general population. *Injury Prevention*, 20, 317-321.

Houtsma, C., & Anestis, M. D. (2017). Practical capability: the impact of handgun ownership among suicide attempt survivors. *Psychiatry Research*, 258, 88-92.

Kaplan, M. S., Adamek, M. E., & Rhoades, J. A. (1998). Prevention of elderly suicide. *American Journal of Preventive Medicine,* 15, 60-64.

Kaplan, M. S., Huguet, N., McFarland, B. H., & Mandle, J. A. (2012). Factors associated with suicide by firearm among U.S. older adult men. *Psychology of Men & Masculinity*, 13, 65-74.

Kaplan, M. S., McFarland, B. H., & Huguet, N. (2009). Characteristics of adult male and female firearm suicide decedents. *Injury Prevention*, 15, 322-327.

Kapusta, N., Etzerdorfer, E., Krall, C., & Sonneck, G. (2007). Firearm legislation reform in the European Union. *British Journal of Psychiatry*, 191, 253-257.

Kellermann, A. L., Rivara, F. P., Somes, G., Reay, D. T., Francisco, J., Banton, J. G., Prodzinski, J., Fligner, C., & Hackman, B. B. (1992). Suicide in the home in relation to gun ownership. *New England Journal of Medicine*, 327, 467-472.

Khazem, L. R., Houtsma, C., Gratz, K. L., Tull, M. T., Green, B. A., & Anestis, M. D. (2016). Firearms matter. *Military Psychology*, 28, 25-33.

Killias, M. (1993). International correlations between gun ownership and rates of homicide and suicide. *Canadian Medical Association Journal*, 148, 1721-1725.

Killias, M., van Kesteren, J., & Rindlisbacher, M. (2001). Guns, violent crime, and suicide in 21 countries. *Canadian Journal of Criminology*, 43, 429-448.

Klieve, H., Barnes, M., & De Leo, D. (2009). Controlling firearms use in Australia. *Social Psychiatry & Psychiatric Epidemiology*, 44, 285-292.

Kposowa, A., Hamilton, D., & Wang, K. (2016). Impact of firearms availability and gun regulation on state suicide rates. *Suicide & Life-Threatening Behavior*, 46, 678-696.

Lahti, A., Keränen, S., Hakko, H., Riala, K., & Räsänen, P. (2014). Northern excess in adolescent male firearm suicides. *European Child & Adolescent Psychiatry*, 23, 45-52.

Lester, D. (1989). Use of handguns and long guns in suicide and homicide. *Psychological Reports,* 65, 938.

Lester, D. (1998a). The use of long guns for murder. *Perceptual & Motor Skills, 87,* 162.

Lester, D. (1988b). *Why women kill themselves*. Springfield, IL: Charles Thomas.

Lester, D. (1990). The availability of firearms and the use of firearms for suicide. *Acta Psychiatrica Scandinavica*, 81, 146-147.

Lester, D., & Frank, M. L. (1988). Handguns, long guns, and suicide. *Psychological Reports, 63,* 606.

Lester, D., & Stack, S. (Eds.) (2015). *Suicide as a dramatic performance*. New Brunswick, NJ: Transaction.

Loftin, C., McDowall, D., Wiersema, B., & Cottey, T. J. (1991). Effects of restrictive licensing of handguns on homicide and suicide in the District of Columbia. *New England Journal of Medicine*, 325, 1615-1620.

Lubin, G., Werbeloff, N., Halperin, D., Shmushkevitch, M., Weiser, M., & Knobler, H. Y. (2010). Decrease in suicide rates after a change of policy reducing access to firearms in adolescents. *Suicide & Life-Threatening Behavior*, 40, 421-424.

Ludwig, J., & Cook, P. J. (2000). Homicide and suicide rates associated with implementation of the Brady Handgun Violence Prevention Act. *Journal of the American Medical Association*, 284, 585-591.

Marks, A., & Stokes, C. S. (1976). Socialization, firearms, and suicide. *Social Problems*, 23, 622-629.

McCarten, J. M., Hoffmire, C. A., & Bossarte, R. M. (2015). Changes in overall and firearm veteran suicide rates by gender, 2001-2010. *American Journal of Preventive Medicine*, 48, 360-364.

Medoff, M. H., & Magadinno, J. P. (1983). Suicides and firearm control laws. *Evaluation Review,* 7, 357-372.

Miller, M., Barber, C., Azrael, D., Hemenway, D., & Molnar, B. E. ((2009). Recent psychopathology, suicidal thoughts and suicide attempts in households with and without firearms. *Injury Prevention*, 15, 183-187.

Mundt, R. J. (1990). Gun control and rates of firearm violence in Canada and the United States. *Canadian Journal of Criminology*, 32, 137-154.

Nestadt, P. S., Triplett, P., Fowler, D. R., & Mojtabai, R. (2017). Urban-rural differences in suicide in the state of Maryland. *American Journal of Public Health*, 107, 1548-1553.

Niederkrotenthaler, T. Till, B., Herberth, A., Kapusta, N. D., Voracek, M., Dervic, K., Etzerdorfer, E., & Sonneck, G. (2009). Can media effects counteract legislation reforms? *Journal of Adolescent Health*, 44, 90-93.

Pope, N. D., Slovak, K. L., & Giger, J. T. (2016). Evaluating a training intervention to prepare geriatric case managers to assess for suicide and firearm safety *Educational Gerontology,* 42, 706-716.

Price, J. H., Thompson, A. J., & Dake, J. A. (2004). Factors associated with state variations i9n homicide, suicide, and unintentional firearm deaths. *Journal of Community Health*, 29, 271-283.

Reisch, T., Steffen, T., Habenstein, A., & Tschacher, W. (2013). Changes in suicide rates in Switzerland before and after firearm restriction resulting from the 2003 Army XX1" reform. *American Journal of Psychiatry*, 170, 977-984.

Rich, C. L., Young, J. G., Fowler, R. C., Wagner, J., & Black, N. A. (1990). Guns and suicide. *American Journal of Psychiatry*, 147, 342-346.

Sanaei-Zadeh, H., Ghorbani, M., Ghanizadeh, A., & Amiri, A. (2004). Suicide by firearm, a unique pattern from Iran. *Archives of Suicide Research*, 8, 173-177.

Sarma, K., & Kola, S. (2010a). Firearm suicide decedents in the Republic of Ireland, 1980-2005. *Public Health*, 124, 273-283.

Sarma, K., & Kola, S. (2010b). Firearms, hanging and drowning suicides in the Republic of Ireland. *Crisis*, 31, 69-75.

Shah, S., Hoffman, R. E., Wake, L., & Marine, W. H. (2000). Adolescent suicide and household access to firearms in Colorado. *Journal of Adolescent Health*, 26, 157-163.

Siegel, M., & Rothman, E. F. (2016). Firearm ownership and suicide rates among US men and women, 1981-2013. *American Journal of Public Health*, 106, 1316-1322.

Simon, R., Chouinard, M., & Gravel, C. (1996). Suicide and firearms. In J. McIntosh (Ed.) *Suicide '96*. Washington, DC: American Association of Suicidology, 35-37.

Slater, G. Y. (2011). The missing piece. *Suicide & Life-Threatening Behavior*, 41, 474-490.

Sloan, J. H., Rivara, F. P., Reay, D. T., Feris, J. A. J., & Kellerman, A. L. (1990). Firearm regulation and rates of suicide. *New England Journal of Medicine*, 322, 369-373.

Slovak, K., & Brewer, T. W. (2010). Suicide and firearm means restriction. *Suicide & Life-Threatening Behavior,* 40, 63-73.

Smith, P. M., Currier, J., & Drescher, K. (2015). Firearm ownership in veterans entering residential PTSD treatment. *Psychiatry Research*, 229, 220-224.

Snowdon, J., & Harris, L. (1992). Firearm suicides in Australia. *Medical Journal of Australia*, 156, 79-83.

Sorenson, S. B, & Vittes, K. A. (2008). Mental health and firearms in community-based surveys. *Evaluation Review*, 32, 239-256.

Stack, S. (2015a). Methods of suicide around the world. In D. Lester & S. Stack (Eds.) *Suicide as a dramatic performance*, pp. 243-255. New Brunswick, NJ: Transaction.

Stack, S. (2015b). The location of the suicidal act. In D. Lester & S. Stack (Eds.) *Suicide as a dramatic performance*, pp. 73-75. New Brunswick, NJ: Transaction.

Stack, S. (2015c). Back to nature. In D. Lester & S. Stack (Eds.) *Suicide as a dramatic performance*, pp. 109-128. New Brunswick, NJ: Transaction.

Stack, S. (2015d). Have gun, will travel. In D. Lester & S. Stack (Eds.) *Suicide as a dramatic performance*, pp. 211-222. New Brunswick, NJ: Transaction.

Stack, S., & Bowman, B. (2015). Suicide in the Grand Canyon National Park. In D. Lester & S. Stack (Eds.) *Suicide as a dramatic performance*, pp. 129-149. New Brunswick, NJ: Transaction.

Stanley, I. H., Hom, M. A., Rogers, M. L., Anestis, M. A., & Joiner, T. E. (2017). Discussing firearm ownership and access as part of suicide risk assessment and prevention. *Archives of Suicide Research*, 21, 237-253.

Tait, G., & Carpenter, B. (2009). Firearm suicide in Queensland. *Journal of Sociology*, 46, 83-98.

Tewksbury, R., Suresh, G., & Holmes, R. M. (2010). Factors related to suicide via firearms and hanging and leaving of suicide notes. *International Journal of Men's Health*, 9, 40-49.

Vars, F. E., McCullumsmith, C. B., Shelton, R. C., & Cropsey, K. L. (2017). Willingness of mentally ill individuals to sign up for a novel proposal to prevent firearm suicide. *Suicide & Life-Threatening Behavior,* 47, 483-492.

Vriniotis, M., Barber, C., Frank, E., Demicco, M. & the New Hampshire Firearm Safety Coalition (2015). A suicide prevention campaign for firearm dealers in New Hampshire. *Suicide & Life-Threatening Behavior*, 45, 157-163.

Watkins, A. M., & Lizotte, A. J. (2011). Does household gun access increase the risk of attempted suicide? *Youth & Society*, 45, 324-346.

Webster, D. W., Vernick, J. S., Zeoli, A. M., & Manganello, J. M. (2004). Association between youth-focused firearm laws and youth suicides. *Journal of the American Medical Association,* 292, 594-601.

Wintemute, G. J. (1988). Handgun availability and firearm mortality. *Lancet*, ii, 1136-1137.

Wright, M. A., Wintemute, G. J., & Claire B. E. (2008). Gun suicide by young people in California. *Journal of Adolescent Health*, 43, 619-622.

Zerling, C., Lynch, C. F., Burmeister, L. F., & Goertz, U. (1993). The choice of weapons in firearm suicides in Iowa. *American Journal of Public Health*, 83, 1630-1632.

In: Firearms and Suicide
Editor: David Lester
ISBN: 978-1-53614-690-5


*Chapter 3*

# WORKING WITH GUN OWNERS, DEALERS AND GUN LOBBYING GROUPS: IS IT HELPFUL OR HARMFUL?

***John F. Gunn III****
Department of Family Science and Human Development
Montclair State University, New Jersey, US

## ABSTRACT

Given the high rates of suicide by firearm in the United States, the partnership between the American Foundation for Suicide Prevention (AFSP) and the National Shooting Sports Foundation (NSSF) appeared off-putting and dangerous to many who, subsequently, voiced strong opposition to what they perceived would be undue influence of the gun lobby on the largest suicide prevention organization in the United States. However, are such partnerships unheard of and how can they be implemented effectively? This chapter seeks to address those questions by reviewing some of the various ways the suicide prevention community and the firearm-owning community have worked together in the past, as well as providing a rationale for effective ways to work together in the future. Although acknowledging the concerns put forward by those concerned

* Corresponding Author Email: Gunnj3@montclair.edu.

with the AFSP/NSSF partnership, this chapter draws attention to the fact that, in order to reduce firearm suicide, it is likely necessary to work with those who can influence the firearm owning community.

In August 2016 the American Foundation for Suicide Prevention (AFSP) announced that it would be joining forces with the National Shooting Sports Foundation (NSSF) in order to help reduce the death rate from suicide by 20 percent by 2025 (Project 2025).

[1] While some viewed this partnership as innocuous, there was immediate concern raised over the importance of gun control in the prevention of suicide. The NSSF opposes measures to enact gun legislation and has advocated for gun ownership in their role as the lobbying arm of the firearm industry (Valentine, 2013). Shortly after the formation of the partnership between AFSP and NSSF, reports began to surface of censorship at the AFSP Out of Darkness Walks[2] and the exclusion of gun legislation groups, such as the Brady Campaign, from participating (Dunkerly, 2017).

However, putting aside the accusations surrounding the partnerships of AFSP and NSSF, the question that I would like to address in this chapter is whether or not partnerships with gun owners, gun dealers, and gun lobbying groups is good or bad for the suicide prevention community? Throughout this chapter I will discuss what has been done and how it has worked and then make some conjectures about the likelihood of success for the partnership between AFSP and NSSF.

Before proceeding to these discussions, it is important that I lay my cards on the table concerning my own position within the shooting community. I grew up in a home that owned guns. From my childhood through my young adulthood, I was an active member in the shooting sport community, I was a lifetime NRA member (although I have resigned my membership), and I still own guns to this day. However, that being said, I am also a strong advocate for gun legislation and, as has often been pointed out by my more conservative friends, I am a "bleeding heart liberal." It is

---

[1]https://afsp.org/campaigns/project-2025/?utm_source=All+Subscribers&utm_campaign=d8f74fd79e-hope_hub_october_17&utm_medium=email&utm_term=0_3fbf9113af-d8f74fd79e-.

[2]https://afsp.donordrive.com/index.cfm?fuseaction=cms.page&id=1196&eventGroupID=9AA117B3-F522-BB6D-359D1AA2D75A7958

from this duel position of gun-owner and liberal academic that I engage in this discussion of the role of gun owners, dealers, and lobbying groups in the prevention of suicide.

## THE RELATIONSHIP BETWEEN FIREARMS AND SUICIDE

Before progressing to a discussion of the various ways suicide prevention advocates have attempted to work with gun groups, it is important to discuss some of the literature examining the relationship between firearms and suicide. Generally speaking, the literature on the relationship between suicide and firearms can be divided into three areas: (1) the lethality of the method, (2) the role of gun ownership on the risk of suicide, and (3) the impact of means restriction on suicide. For the sake of brevity, I will delve only briefly into these areas since other chapters in this book will provide greater detail about some of these topics.[3]

### Firearm Lethality

The relationship between suicide and firearms can be most clearly understood by considering the lethality of this specific method. Looking at a large number of suicides across several states, Spicer and Miller (2000) found that certain methods, such as poisoning, were the most common method for those surviving a suicide attempt, but that firearms were the most common method for those dying by suicide. This finding was further supported by Shenassa, Catlin and Buka (2003). In an examination of suicides from 1990 through 1997, they found that suicidal behavior involving firearms was 2.6 times deadlier than the next closest lethal method (suffocation). They also estimated that preventing access to firearms would reduce the proportion of fatal firearm suicides by roughly 32% for minors and 6.5% for adults.

---

[3] See Chapters 1 and 2.

More recently, Anestis (2013) examined suicide in the military and concluded that part of the increased rate of suicide among military personnel when compared to the general population was a by-product of the greater proportion of suicidal behavior using firearms. As a result of the greater lethality of firearms, those who engage in suicidal behavior with a firearm are more likely than those using other methods to die on their first attempt (Anestis, 2016). While those working in suicide prevention would surely want to identify and make contact with those considering suicide *prior to* an attempt, there is more often an opportunity to provide care and support *following* a non-fatal suicidal behavior. This opportunity is not often present among those engaging in suicidal behavior with a firearm, since their first attempt often represents their last as a result of the higher lethality associated with this method.

## Gun Ownership and Suicide

The relationship between gun ownership and suicide rates has a relatively long history of research in suicidology. Lester (1989), using the circulation of firearm magazines as an index of gun ownership, found that, while homicide rates were not related to this measure of ownership, suicide rates by firearm and suicide rates in general were higher in those states whose gun ownership was greater. Availability of a firearm in the home has also been linked to increased risk of suicide occurring (Kellerman, et al., 1992), and this finding has also been supported at the national level, with gun ownership related to national suicide rates (Killias, 1993).

More recently, these findings have been further supported. Miller, Warren, Hemenway and Azrael (2013) found that rates of firearm ownership were correlated with the overall suicide rate and firearm suicide rates but not with non-firearm suicide rates. These findings were not greatly affected by gender, age or race. Siegel and Rothman (2016) examined suicide rates across all 50 American states from 1981 to 2013. Their findings supported a strong relationship between gun ownership and suicide by firearm. Finally, evidence from Anestis and Houtsma (2017) indicates that firearm ownership is a strong predictor of suicide rates even when controlling for a number of other well-established risk factors for suicide.

## Working with Gun Owners

Perhaps the clearest way in which the suicide prevention community can and has worked with gun owners is through the use of educational programs that influence the storage practices of gun owners. I will discuss the evidence concerning safe storage of firearms and death by suicide, but first it is important to discuss the nature of safe storage in the United States. Schuster and colleagues (2000), drawing on information from the 1994 National Health Interview Survey and its 2000 supplement, found that, of those reporting having at least one firearm in the home, 43% had at least one firearm that was not locked up. Across all homes reporting ownership of a firearm, 9% reported keeping a firearm unlocked and loaded, and 4% reported keeping them unlocked, unloaded, but stored with the ammunition. While this represents 13% of homes with unsafe storage, there were safe storage practices in 39% of homes (i.e., firearms were locked and unloaded, and the ammunition was stored separately).

More recently, Crifasi and colleagues (2018), in a nationally representative sample of gun owners, found that only 46% reported safe storage practices, and that variables associated with this safe storage included having children in the home, owning only handguns, and having attended gun safety courses. Also of interest was the finding that gun owners reported law enforcement, hunting or outdoor groups, active-duty military, and the National Rifle Association as the most effective at communicating safe storage practices. Rowhani-Rahbar and colleagues (2018) found that approximately 61% of firearm owners report having received firearms training. However, only 15% of those surveyed reported that their training included any suicide prevention material.

Evidence has suggested that keeping a firearm locked, unloaded, and having ammunition also locked and stored in a separate location, can serve a protective function against suicide among youth (Grossman, et al., 2005).

Khazem and colleagues (2016) found that unsafe firearm storage was associated with increased fearlessness about death (a risk factor for suicide) and that firearm storage practices served as a moderator between suicide ideation and the self-reported likelihood of engaging in future suicidal behavior. As a result of this increased risk, Simon (2007) recommended that any patients reporting suicidal thoughts or behaviors to a clinician should be asked if they possess firearms and that efforts to remove firearms from the home should be undertaken.

However, there is debate about whether or not safe-storage campaigns can be effective in increasing the safe storage of firearms. In Washington state, Sidman and colleagues (2005) did not find any support for a safe-storage campaign that included television and radio announcements, educational materials, billboards, and discount coupons for lock boxes. Despite these findings, there has been some evidence that safe-storage information can have an impact. Barkin and colleagues (2008) targeted the primary caregivers of children aged 2 to 11 years through their pediatric offices. They found that safe storage of firearms increased among families exposed to educational information about use of storage locks for firearms. Further evidence has also suggested that similar educational approaches are effective with general practitioners as well, with increased safe storage exhibited among those educated on the topic by family doctors (Albright & Burge, 2003). Caron (2004) looked at the enactment of the Canadian Firearms Act in 1992. Findings support safe-storage measures in reducing suicides by firearm. However, contrary to previous work, Caron found that suicide by other methods subsequently increased. Horn and colleagues (2003) examined the effect of distributing gun safes and trigger locks to a sample of gun owners in Alaska. Findings indicated that, when supplied with a safe, gun-owners were more likely to store safely, but that gun locks were less effective at changing the behavior of gun-owners.[4]

[4] A gun lock is a mechanical device that disables use by stopping the action/slide of the firearm from going forward and making it impossible to load with ammunition.

## GUN DEALERS AND LOBBYING GROUPS

While education programs can be effective means of reducing suicide among gun owners, they are only part of the solution. For a more wide-spread impact, it may be necessary to work more closely with gun dealers and lobbying groups. As discussed in the introduction to this chapter, the recent partnership between AFSP and NSSF has resulted in a great deal of controversy. However, this is certainly not the first partnership between gun advocacy groups, dealers, and the suicide prevention community. Recently, Barber, Frank and Demicco (2017) outlined the various ways in which health professionals can and have worked with gun advocacy groups and gun retailers. Some of the various partnerships they discuss, and others not mentioned, include:

- Firearm retailers, gun rights advocates, public health and mental health professionals formed the New Hampshire Firearm Safety Coalition. This resulted in the distribution of posters and brochures to gun shops concerning suicide prevention which included temporary removal of firearms from the homes of those at risk of suicide and safe storage/locking.
- The Maryland Licensed Firearm Dealer's Association (MLFDA), after being contacted by a mental health advocate, voted unanimously to include a suicide prevention link on the organizations Internet homepage.
- The Utah Shooting Sports Council, state agency representatives, firearm instructors, and suicide researchers created a suicide prevention module for firearm instructors which was adopted as part of the curriculum for concealed-carry permit seekers.
- In Washington State, the region's NRA lobbyist (Second Amendment Foundation), policy makers, and suicide prevention experts formed a partnership to prevent firearm suicide. This partnership (Forefront) created a *Safer Homes, Suicide Aware* campaign that targeted safer storage practices for firearms as well as medications.

- In Nevada gun shows include suicide prevention displays.
- Harvard School of Public Health's *Means Matter* initiative looks to educate on safe storage and removal of means and, thereby, reducing suicide through the limiting of access to lethal means.

Runyan and colleagues (2017) surveyed law enforcement agencies and gun retailers to determine if there was a willingness to provide for the temporary removal of firearms in the case of suicide risk. Both types of organizations surveyed reported already offering these services, with three quarters of law enforcement agencies offering this service and 47.6% of gun retailers. This indicates the potential of working with organizations such as these in promoting safe storage practices. Recently, Branas and colleagues (2017) outlined a number of recommendations for future work to combat the firearm crisis in the United States that came out of a national meeting of public health and gun violence prevention advocates in 2016. In addition to calling for greater research, working with state legislators, and developing a business plan, they recommended working in collaboration with firearm owners, firearm manufacturers, police, pro-firearm advocates, and a number of other organizations, as well as promoting safety as a way of bridging the political divide created by the gun debate.

As can be seen, partnership between organizations with public health and suicide prevention goals and organizations opposed to gun control measures can be achieved and has been successful on a state-by-state level. The partnership between the AFSP and NSSF represents a similar partnership to those discussed above but on a much larger scale. As previously mentioned, AFSP's Project 2025 initiative has set a goal of reducing the annual suicide rate by 20% by the year 2025.[5] Citing the fact that half of all American suicides are by firearms and that previous efforts to reduce the firearm suicide rate have failed to have an impact, AFSP presented their partnership with NSSF as a new approach to an ongoing

[5] https://afsp.org/campaigns/project-2025/?utm_source=All+Subscribers&utm_campaign=d8f74fd79e-hope_hub_october_17&utm_medium=email&utm_term=0_3fbf9113af-d8f74fd79e-

problem.[6] AFSP outlined their rationale for this partnership in several ways, including:

- Working with NSSF will allow for the dissemination of suicide prevention education to thousands of gun retail stores, shooting ranges, and gun owners across the nation.
- This education will focus on risk factors and warning signs as well as the actions needed such as temporary removal of firearms from homes during periods of risk, safe storage, and retailers denying sales when suicide risk is suspected.
- AFSP maintained that no funding is being received from NSSF, firearm manufacturers, or gun lobbying organizations and that AFSP is, likewise, not providing funds to these groups.

Despite this, there has been growing reports about the silencing of gun control advocates at AFSP sponsored events. Dunkerly (2017) outlined her experiences following the formation of the AFSP/NSSF partnership in an op-ed for the *New York Times*. In it, Dunkerly detailed how, after the formation of the partnership, she and others were instructed not to be vocal about gun control. She also detailed how organizations that advocated for gun control were excluded from participation in the *Out of Darkness* walks sponsored by AFSP. This eventually, according to Dunkerly, lead to the removal of one co-chairwomen and her own removal as chairwomen of the Pasadena walk and her removal from the Greater Los Angeles AFSP Chapter board. Wilson (2017) also detailed experiences with censorship at AFSP-sponsored events following the partnership between AFSP and NSSF. Wilson, who works with Maine Gun Safety Coalition[7] based in Portland, detailed how, three days prior to presenting on safe storage practices at the AFSP *Out of Darkness* walk in Portland, the talk was canceled. When AFSP was pressed for answers as to why, Wilson stated that he was told that the

[6] https://afsp.org/about-suicide/firearms-and-suicide-prevention/firearms-and-suicide-prevention-program/.

[7] http://www.mainegunsafety.org/.

decision to exclude them was due to concern that it would be construed by gun rights groups as supporting gun control.

McGlone (2017) also reported on the exclusion of gun control groups from distributing pamphlets at AFSP walks. Moms Demand Action for Gun Sense and the Brady Campaign had both intended on participating in the event and distributing pamphlets, but they were informed that they would be unable to participate. The regional director for AFSP, Jessica van der Stad, who is quoted in the piece, cited the legislative stance of the organizations as the reason for their exclusion from the event. While these descriptions of silencing gun control advocates at AFSP sponsored events is certainly troubling, it is important to point out that these are opinion pieces and anecdotal. In reading through the news reports on these topics, it is also apparent that they are describing the same events (e.g., the San Diego Walk and the Portland Walk) and, therefore, may represent isolated cases.

## Barriers to Collaboration

What has hopefully become apparent so far in this chapter is that collaboration with gun groups can open the door to the prevention of suicides using firearms and, through targeting this method, assist in the reduction of the overall suicide rate. However, while we have discussed various ways in which suicide prevention advocates have coordinated with these groups, we have not discussed the barriers to successful collaboration. This section will review some of these barriers and how they might be overcome.

Perhaps the single greatest barrier to collaboration is the ideological divide between those advocating for gun ownership and those advocating for more stringent gun control measures. This gulf is made all the more difficult to navigate given the gun culture of the United States. Kocsis (2015), in discussing gun ownership in the United States from a philosophical standpoint, argued that conflict within the United States over gun ownership is a clashing of various American ideals, such as the ideals of liberty, property rights, and protection from the state versus the freedom that can be enjoyed from safety from gun violence. Kalesan and colleagues (2016) examined what they called the *social gun culture*. Here, participants were asked to assess what their friends and family would think of them if they did not own firearms. Findings indicated that there was a strong association between perceptions of how friends and family would view them for not owning guns and gun ownership.

Stroebe, Leander and Kruglanski (2017) found that those who own guns are more likely to perceive their work as dangerous and to perceive the threat of assault to be more likely. Other evidence points to the growing polarization of politics in the United States, with gun ownership becoming a salient feature of those voting Republican (Joslyn, et al., 2017). Richards (2017) found further evidence for the role of political partisanship in the gun culture of the United States. Both political contributions from lobbying groups (such as the NRA) and the breakdown of distinct voter groups (e.g., hunters) were predictive of votes and sponsorship of gun bills among the House of Representatives members.

I have thus far touched on a number of academic works that examine the political ideology and cultural divide that makes collaboration difficult, but I would like to conclude with anecdotal evidence from my own life as an academic, liberal, and gun owner. As I stated in the introduction to this chapter, I grew up in a gun owning home and was active in the shooting community for much of my childhood and through young adulthood. My experiences in this community were enjoyable and, not sharing the political ideologies of those in the community, it was also informative about the differences in thought on both sides. Among those I grew up with, any media that was not conservative was viewed, at best, as suspect. Academics were viewed, generally, as liberal propagandists whose findings were skewed by their political ideology. I want to be clear that these are my experiences of this community which may not be the same as others.

# Conclusion

I have set out in this chapter to discuss the efforts by the suicide prevention community to work alongside the gun owning and advocacy community. What I hope is apparent is the need for collaboration across multiple groups. Suicide prevention cannot succeed if groups, such as AFSP, do not reach across the vast political divide to gun owners and advocacy groups. I am certainly not advocating for abandoning gun legislation. Gun violence in the United States is a major public health concern and one that must be targeted through legislation. That being said, suicide prevention advocates will not succeed in reaching firearm owners if they attempt to reach them alone. Evidence by social scientists points to the ideological divide that makes it difficult for outsiders to reach this community. My own anecdotal experiences within the shooting community makes it clear to me that we need support from those trusted by this community if we are to succeed at preventing suicide by firearm. I outline a number of recommendations below that I believe to be essential for suicide prevention among the firearm owning community.

## Recommendations

- Advocating for family physicians and general practitioners to discuss gun ownership and safe storage with patients can help to increase safe storage practices.
- Collaboration with gun advocacy groups is the key to reaching the gun community (i.e., owners, retailers, and gun ranges). Suicide prevention advocates should be open to working with gun retailers and organizations, and they should make efforts to reach out to these groups.
- Advocacy for safe storage education and legislation is likely to be more effectively collaborated on than other forms of gun legislation. This is not to say other forms of legislation should be avoided, but

that safe storage education will be more likely to be successful in our politically divided environment.

## References

Albright, T. L, & Burge, S. K. (2003). Improving firearm storage habits: Impact of brief office counseling by family physicians. *Journal of the American Board of Family Medicine, 16,* 40-46.

Anestis, M. D. (2013). Means and capacity for suicidal behavior: A comparison of the ratio of suicide attempts and deaths by suicide in the US military and general population. *Journal of Affective Disorders, 148,* 42-47.

Anestis, M. D. (2016). Prior suicide attempts are less common in suicide decedents who died by firearms relative to those who died by other means. *Journal of Affective Disorders, 189,* 106-109.

Barber, C., Frank, E., & Demicco, R. (2017). Reducing suicides through partnerships between health professionals and gun owner groups – Beyond docs vs glocks. *JAMA Internal Medicine, 177,* 5-6.

Barkin, S. L., Finch, S. A., Ip, E. H., Scheindlin, B., Craig, J. A., Steffes, J., & Wasserman, R. C. (2008). Is office-based counseling about media use, timeouts, and firearm storage effective? Results from a cluster-randomized, controlled trial. *Pediatrics, 122,* e15-e25.

Branas, C. C., Flescher, A., Formica, M. K., Galea, S., Hennig, N., Liller, K. D., Madanat, H. N., & Ying, J. (2017). Academic public health and the firearm crisis: An agenda for action. *American Journal of Public Health, 107,* e1-e3.

Caron, J. (2004). Gun control and suicide: Possible impact of Canadian legislation to ensure safe storage of firearms. *Archives of Suicide Research, 8,* 361-371.

Crifasi, C. K., Doucette, M. L., McGinty, E. E., Webster, D. W., & Barry, C. L. (2018). Storage practices of US gun owners in 2016. *American Journal of Public Health, 108,* 532-537.

Dunkerly, E. (2017, December 26). The gun lobby is hindering suicide prevention. *The New York Times,* retrieved from https://www.nytimes.com/2017/12/26/opinion/gun-lobby-suicide-prevention.html.

Grossman, D. C., Mueller, B. A., Riedy, C., Dowd, M. D., Villaveces, A., Prodzinski, J., & Harruff, R. (2005). Gun storage practices and risk of youth suicide and unintentional firearm injuries. *JAMA,* 293, 707-714.

Horn, A., Grossman, D. C., Jones, W., & Berger, L. R. (2003). Community based program to improve firearm storage practices in rural Alaska. *Injury Prevention, 9,* 231-234.

Joslyn, M. R., Haider-Markel, D. P., Baggs, M., & Bilbo, A. (2017). Emerging political identities? Gun ownership and voting in presidential elections. *Social Science Quarterly, 98,* 382-396.

Kalesan, B., Villarreal, M. D., Keyes, K. M., & Galea, S. (2016). Gun ownership and social gun culture. *Injury Prevention, 22,* 216-220.

Kellerman, A. L., Rivara, F. P., Somes, G., Reay, D. T., Francisco, J., Banton, J. G., & Hackman, B. B. (1992). Suicide in the home in relation to gun ownership. *The New England Journal of Medicine, 327,* 467-472.

Khazem, L. R., Houtsma, C., Gratz, K. L., Tull, M. T., Green, B. A., & Anestis, M. D. (2016). Firearms matter: The moderating role of firearm storage in the association between current suicidal ideation and likelihood of future suicide attempts among United States military personnel. *Military Psychology, 28,* 25-33.

Killias, M. (1993). International correlations between gun ownership and rates of homicide and suicide. *Canadian Medical Association Journal, 148,* 1721-1725.

Kocsis, M. (2015). Gun ownership and gun culture in the United States of America. *Essays in Philosophy, 16,* 154-179.

Lester, D. (1989). Gun ownership and suicide in the United States. *Psychological Medicine, 19,* 519-521.

McGlone, A. (2017, October 27). Suicide prevention walk organizers tell gun control advocates to keep away. *Voice of San Diego,* retrieved from https://www.voiceofsandiego.org/topics/nonprofits/gun-control-advocates-kept-out-suicide-walk/.

Miller, M., Warren, M., Hemenway, D., & Azrael, D. (2015). Firearms and suicide in US cities. *Injury Prevention, 21,* e116-e119.

Richards, R. (2017). The role of interest groups and group interests on gun legislation in the U.S. house. *Social Science Quarterly, 98,* 471-484.

Rowhani-Rahbar, A., Lyons, V. H., Simonetti, J. A., Azrael, D., & Miller, M. (2018). Formal firearm training among adults in the USA: results of a national survey. *Injury Prevention, 24*, 161-165.

Runyan, C. W., Brooks-Russell, A., Brandspigel, S., Betz, M., Tung, G., Novins, D., & Agans, R. (2017). Law enforcement and gun retailers as partners for safely storing guns to prevent suicide: A study in 8 mountain west states. *American Journal of Public Health, 107,* 1789-1794.

Schuster, M. A., Franke, T. M., Bastian, A. M., Sor, S., & Halfon, N. (2000). Firearm storage patterns in US homes with children. *American Journal of Public Health, 90,* 588-594.

Shenassa, E. D., Catlin, S. N., & Buka, S. L. (2003). Lethality of firearms relative to other suicide methods: A population based study. *Journal of Epidemiology & Community Health, 57,* 120-124.

Sidman, E., Grossman, D. C., Koepsell, T., D'Ambrosio, L., Britt, J., Simpson, E. S., Rivara, F. P., & Bergman, A. B. (2005). Evaluation of a community-based handgun safe-storage campaign. *Pediatrics, 115,* e654-e661.

Siegel, M., & Rothman, E. F. (2016). Firearm ownership and suicide rates among US men and women, 1981-2013. *American Journal of Public Health, 106,* 1316-1322.

Simon, R. I. (2007). Gun safety management with patients at risk for suicide. *Suicide & Life-Threatening Behavior, 37,* 518-526.

Spicer, R. S., & Miller, T. R. (2000). Suicide acts in 8 states: Incidence and case fatality rates by demographics and method. *American Journal of Public Health, 90,* 1885-1891.

Stroebe, W., Leander, N. P., & Kruglanski, A. W. (2017). Is it a dangerous world out there? The motivational bases of American gun ownership. *Personality & Social Psychology Bulletin, 43,* 1071-1085.

Valentine, M. (2013, September 12). The gun lobbying group you don't hear about. *The Atlantic,* retrieved from https://www.theatlantic.

com/national/archive/2013/09/the-gun-lobbying-group-you-dont-hear-about/279616/.

Wilson, N. (2017, November 24). Main compass: For gun owners, suicide prevention needs to be a collaborative effort. *Central Maine,* retrieved from https://www.centralmaine.com/2017/11/24/maine-compass-for-gun-owners-suicide-prevention-needs-to-be-a-collaborative-effort/.

In: Firearms and Suicide
Editor: David Lester
ISBN: 978-1-53614-690-5


*Chapter 4*

# Firearms Control: What Works? What Does Not? Some Lessons from Canada

***Antoon A. Leenaars[1,*], Robert Olson[2] and Karin Lavoie[2]***
[1]Private Practice, Windsor, Canada,
[2]Center for Suicide Prevention, Calgary, Canada

## Abstract

Public health organizations have recommended restricted access and safe storage practices as means to reduce firearms injuries and deaths, most specifically, suicide, homicide and accidental deaths. We examine the effects of three firearms restrictions on suicide in Canada. Canada's Criminal Amendment Act in 1977 (Bill C-51) mandated strict licensing and restricted availability of firearms, such as handguns. A subsequent bill (Bill C-17) tightened firearms acquisitions (FAC). The last bill (Bill C-68) required people to register all shotguns and rifles. There was significant opposition to Bill C-68, unlike the former laws, by diverse groups such as Indigenous people, farmers, gun lobbyists, and hunters. The law was eventually repealed in Parliament. Research shows that Bill C-51 and Bill C-17 did have significant impacts on firearm suicides. In conclusion, we

* Corresponding Author Email: draalee@sympatico.ca.

address the question: "Do the lessons in Canada mean anything for the United States of America and elsewhere around the world?"

One strategy for suicide prevention that has a prevailing consensus is that a public health approach can be effective in preventing suicide and, in particular, means restriction is useful (Stengel, 1964; Kreitman, 1976; Leenaars, Cantor, Connolly et al., 2000; World Health Organization [WHO], 2002, 2006). Public health organizations have recommended restricted access and safe storage practices as means to reduce firearm injuries and deaths, specifically suicide, homicide, and accidental deaths. Focusing on suicide, we aim to present the effects of three laws in Canada restricting firearms. Canada's Criminal Amendment Act in 1977 (Bill C-51) mandated strict licensing and restricted the availability of firearms, such as handguns. A subsequent bill (Bill C-17) tightened firearm acquisitions (FAC). The last bill (Bill C-68) required people to register all shotguns and rifles.

Erwin Stengel (1964) was one of the first in the last century to propose a public health approach as a means for decreasing the incidence of suicide, noting, for example, that the detoxification of domestic gas (from coal gas with high carbon monoxide content to natural gas) might have reduced the suicide rates in nations where the switch had taken place. Subsequent research on the detoxification of domestic gas in England supported Stengel's proposal (Kreitman, 1976). A comprehensive review of the research around the globe supports the approach more generally, often called *controlling the environment* (Leenaars, Cantor, Connolly et al., 2000). After careful analysis of all measures by an international team of researchers, headed by Bertolote (1993), tactics to prevent suicide that had support in the empirical literature were proposed. Among the tactics were gun possession control, detoxification of domestic gas, detoxification of car emissions and control of toxic substance availability. Gun control legislation, among this list, is often cited as the prototypical example of public health intervention to prevent suicide (Bertolote, 1993; Leenaars, DeLeo, Goldney et al., 1998; WHO, 2006). Gun control is, for example, an excellent example because guns are a lethal method and easy availability obviously can facilitate death.

One would predict that availability would increase suicide and that stricter gun laws would reduce the suicide rate. There are ample laws, for example, in Australia, Canada, New Zealand, Norway, and the United States (USA) which facilitate scientific investigation. However, this chapter reviews the research on the association of the availability of the means, guns and suicide, and on the effect of gun control legislation or laws on suicide in Canada.

Within a public health perspective, of course, one can study the association between firearms and suicide at the individual level and population (or ecological) level. Each has limitations, but also benefits. Individual (case-control) empirical studies have the problem of finding reasonable controls and allowing for generalization, often from small groups, to different larger groups. The population level raises the problem of the *ecological fallacy*, drawing conclusions about individuals from groups (aggregate) data. We will examine both levels of study in Canada. However, first, a few reflections on suicide: How can we best understand suicide?

## SUICIDE

What is suicide? It is estimated that 1.6 million people die by violence each year around the world, although, given that known rates are a fraction of the incidences, it is probably closer to 2 million. Almost half (800,000 to 1,000,000) of these are suicides; one-third are homicides (530,000 to 660,000) and one-fifth (320,000 to 400,000) are war-related (WHO, 2002, 2014). (In 2014, the WHO reported a suicide number of 804,000.) Of course, countries vary in the incidence and rate of suicide (and homicide). This is, for example, true about Canada and the USA, despite their close geographical location. It is often assumed that violence is more prevalent in the USA; yet, there is one exception, *suicide*! On the other hand, homicide is much higher in the USA. Table 1 presents the rates of suicide and homicide in Canada and the USA for selected years, largely from data available from the WHO, and with current additions from Statistics Canada, CDC, and SPRC (See Table 1). In 1969, the suicide rate for Canada was

10.9 per 100,000; for the USA it was 11.1. Twenty years later (1988) the respective rates were 13.5 and 12.4. Whereas in 1969, the homicide rate for Canada was 1.8 per 100,000; for the USA, it was 7.7. Twenty years later the respective rates were 1.9 and 8.9. As can be gleaned from Table 1, the most current available rates for both the USA and Canada (2014) suggest that the suicide rate for Canada was 12.0 per 100,000, and for the USA was 13.0. (Since around 2010, the decades-old recorded trend that suicide is lower in the USA, has reversed. Why?) The respective rates for homicide were 1.5 and 4.5. That is a very significant statistical difference!

No single factor or event explains why so many people are violent. Violence is multi-determined. Violence is complex. Suicide, homicide and war-related deaths (the three main types of global violence) are multi-determined and require a multiaxial approach to understand them (Meehl, 1986). This is very true about suicide. Suicide is the result of the interplay of individual, relationship(s), social, cultural and environmental factors. This is sometimes called *the ecological model* (Bronfrenbrenner, 1979; Dahlberg & Krug, 2002; Jenkins & Singh, 2000). First applied to child abuse (Garbarino & Crouter, 1978), the model has been applied to a vast array of behaviors, most recently violence, including self-directed violence; i.e., suicide (WHO, 2002) (see Figure 1).

The model simply suggests that there are different levels, that is, individual, relationship(s), community, and societal, that influence suicide and thus, by implication, one can prevent the behavior at various levels. Comprehensive approaches, therefore, would target not only the individual but also the factors beyond the individual. These approaches are focused on the relationship (e.g., family members, friends, health-providers), community, societal, governmental, and environmental levels. Thus, to best understand and, by implication, control suicide, that our evidence-based science allows, we must take a multi-faceted or multi-dimensional approach (Dahlberg & Krug, 2004; Jenkins, & Singh, 2000; Leenaars, 1988, 2004; Shneidman, 1973a &b, 1985; WHO, 2006).

**Table 1. Suicide and Homicide Rates in Canada and the USA (from the WHO, Statistics Canada, CDC, & SPRC)**

| | Suicide | | Homicide | |
|---|---|---|---|---|
| | Canada | USA | Canada | USA |
| 1969 | 10.9 | 11.1 | 1.8 | 7.7 |
| 1970 | 11.3 | 11.5 | 2.0 | 8.2 |
| 1971 | 11.9 | 11.7 | 2.2 | 9.1 |
| 1972 | 12.2 | 12.0 | 2.3 | 9.4 |
| 1973 | 12.6 | 12.0 | 2.4 | 9.8 |
| 1974 | 12.9 | 12.1 | 2.5 | 10.2 |
| 1975 | 12.4 | 12.7 | 2.7 | 10.0 |
| 1976 | 12.8 | 12.5 | 2.4 | 9.1 |
| 1977 | 14.2 | 13.3 | 2.6 | 9.2 |
| 1978 | 14.8 | 12.5 | 2.5 | 9.4 |
| 1979 | 14.2 | 12.1 | 2.5 | 9.9 |
| 1980 | 14.0 | 11.8 | 2.1 | 10.5 |
| 1981 | 14.0 | 12.0 | 2.3 | 10.2 |
| 1982 | 14.3 | 12.2 | 2.4 | 9.5 |
| 1983 | 15.1 | 12.1 | 2.4 | 8.5 |
| 1984 | 13.7 | 12.4 | 2.3 | 8.2 |
| 1985 | 12.9 | 12.3 | 2.1 | 8.2 |
| 1986 | 13.4 | 12.8 | 2.0 | 8.9 |
| 1987 | 14.0 | 12.7 | 2.2 | 8.6 |
| 1988 | 13.5 | 12.4 | 1.9 | 8.9 |
| 1989 | 12.8 | 12.2 | 2.4 | 8.7 |
| 1990 | 12.2 | 12.5 | 2.4 | 9.4 |
| 1995 | 13.5 | 11.8 | 2.0 | 8.2 |
| 2000 | 11.8 | 10.4 | 1.8 | 5.9 |
| 2005 | 11.6 | 10.9 | 2.1 | 5.9 |
| 2010 | 11.6 | 12.1 | 1.6 | 4.8 |
| 2014 | 12.0 | 13.0 | 1.5 | 4.5 |

Rates are incidence per 100,000.

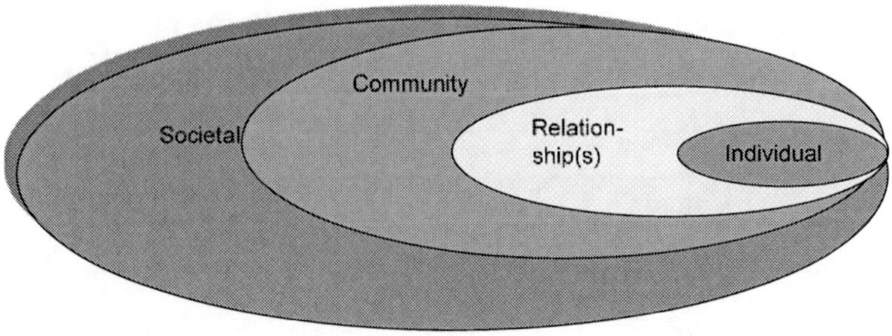


Figure 1. An Ecological Model for Understanding Suicide.

## FIREARMS AND SUICIDE: LITERATURE SEARCH

What is evidence-based research? One accepted method is a systematic literature review (Mann, Apter, Bertolote et al., 2005). Literature reviews on gun control and suicide in Canada have been done before (Leenaars, 2007; Leenaars et al., 2000). For this chapter, electronic searches of all articles available from 1998 to February 14, 2018, were conducted of all literature archived at the Centre for Suicide Prevention (CSP), Calgary, Alberta, Canada. The centre's archive houses over 45,000 documents on the topic of suicide. In addition, we searched for articles targeting systematic reviews. We searched the databases at Medline, Psychology and Behavioural Sciences, and Centre for Suicide Prevention (CSP). We did not *a priori* specify "relevant" journals; we did not exclude any source. We searched the terms "gun control and suicide prevention and Canada"; as well as "firearm regulation and suicide prevention and Canada". From the results, we initially identified fourteen articles. Full texts of all articles that met the criteria were retrieved. (Only one article was located when we searched 2008 to present.) However, three of the 14 articles only noted that it may be an important strategy for Canada, the military (a high risk group), and Nunavut (the territory with the highest risk). Therefore, only eleven articles were actually located (with two by the senior author). Out of the eleven, two presented trends among various countries, which included Canada, showing international trends on firearm availability and suicide; thus, it may be more accurate to state nine, and that may be labeled meager at best. All 14 articles were reviewed in detail, summarized, highlighted and catalogued. We aimed to present our findings below within a larger context of the international literature.

## Gun Availability and Suicide

Briefly, the public health approach (see Leenaars, 2005) to health not only defines, describes, and measures a problem such as suicide ("What is the problem?"), but also studies and analyses the probable cause(s), such as patterns and associations ("What is the cause(s) of the problem?" or "Does availability of a means or mode for the problem make a difference?"), and then studies how to predict and control the problem ("What can we do to stop or reduce the problem?" "Would means restriction help?").

Verification, of course, is a basic in science (Ayer, 1959; Leenaars, Dieserud, Wenckstern, Dyregrov, Lester, & Lyke, 2018; Millon, 2010; Zachar & Kendler, 2010); yet, a theory ("Gun control works") can never be actually verified, only tested/supported. Thus, like almost all of public health (and mental health for that matter), we are left with questions: How do we understand gun control's effectiveness? Does it work? Regrettably, some proponents of gun control have attempted to classify firearms control with robust generalizations "Everything works!" Frankly, these non-evidence-based gun control proponents have aided the right to bear arms advocates, like the NRA, for example. To begin an empirical answer to our question, we present the studies of suicide and gun ownership and suicide and availability of guns.

The availability of guns is difficult to measure, often only indirect measures are available, such as the accidental death rate by firearms and the percentage of firearms used for crimes such as murder (Lester, 2000a). In Canada, by far the largest number of gun related deaths is by suicide, approximately four-fifths of all firearm deaths (Wilkins, 2005). (Homicides account for around 15%, and about 4% involve unintentional [accidental] deaths by firearms.) The main method of suicide in Canada is by hanging, followed by firearms. (In females, the main method is suicide by poisoning, followed by hanging.)

There are only two studies on firearm ownership, as measured by gun licenses, in Canada. Carrington and Moyer (1994) first reported that firearm suicide was associated with ownership in Canada, and Lester (2000b) replicated that finding. Despite only two studies in Canada, Etzersdorfer, Kapusta and Sonneck (2006), Killias (1993), Lester (1988a; 1988b; 1996), and Markush and Bertolucci (1984) found that ownership of firearms in various countries was positively associated with suicide by shooting. Two longitudinal analysis studies of firearm availability in an array of countries (including the USA, Switzerland, Finland, France, Canada, Sweden, Australia, the Netherlands, England and Wales, Scotland, Norway, Spain and New Zealand), support the association between the percentage of households owning firearms and firearm suicide (Killias, van Kesteren, & Rindlishbacher, 2001; Ajdacic-Gross, Killias, Hepp et al., 2006). The international data also showed that the proportion of firearm suicides decreased simultaneously with the decrease in the proportion of homes owning guns. Although these two studies included Canada, specifics on Canada are not presented, only cross-sectional international data.

It may be concluded that there is a strong positive correlation of the rate of gun ownership and firearm suicide in Canada. The next question in public health arose: Would restriction of the means reduce suicides (and violence in general)? (Leenaars, 2006; 2007). Does it work or not?

## Individual Level Studies on Guns and Suicide

To the best of our knowledge, there are no individual level studies in Canada! In other countries, the studies at an individual level "indicate that a gun in the home is significantly associated with a higher risk of suicide, especially among the young" (Miller & Hemenwey, 1999, p. 73). These are also called case-control studies; there are, however, numerous problems with these studies (Leenaars, 2007; Lester, 2000; Miller & Hemenway, 1999). Limitations include the lack of reasonable controls, the presence of confounding factors, and the subjectivity of informants. Be that as it may, there are some beginning, mainly American, studies at the individual level of analysis. Kellerman, Rivera, Somes et al. (1992), in a frequently cited study, found that people who died by suicide were more likely to have a gun in the home. They studied all cases of suicide over 32 months that occurred in the home of the suicide in two urban areas, Shelby County, Tennessee and King County, Washington. They controlled for sex, race, age range, and confounding variables (such as failure to graduate high school, living alone, consumption of alcohol, current medication, hospitalization). After controlling for the confounders, the presence of a gun was significantly associated with the risk of suicide. The risk was higher when the gun was a handgun, loaded, and kept in unlocked storage.

Cummings, Koepsell, Grossman et al. (1997) overcame the common problem of informational bias in case control studies on suicide. They studied the actual handguns present in the home in 353 cases of people who killed themselves during the period of 1980-1992 by analyzing whether the purchase of a gun from a licensed dealer was associated with suicide. They controlled for social factors (confounders) such as income, and education. They showed that the person who died by suicide was more likely to have had a gun and to have purchased a gun compared to matched controls.

Case control (individual) studies by other researchers (Bailey, Kellerman, Somes, et al., 1997; Beautrais, Joyce, & Mulder 1996; Brent, Perper, Goldstein, et al., 1988; Brent, Perper, Allman, 1991; Brent, Perper, Moritz, et al., 1993) have reported the same association. Indeed, Brent et al. (1993) showed statistically that one may be able to generalize the results of individual cases to the community as a whole, not just for adolescents but for the whole population (Lester, 2000; Miller & Hemenway, 1999). Clearly, more studies are needed, especially in Canada.

To conclude, from a public health perspective, the individual case level studies do not allow us to conclude that gun control might work in Canada since no research exists. Cross-cultural verification does not exist in Canada and is lacking around the world. One cannot transpose the results from the USA to Canada (and to other countries) without a great deal of caution. (We will address the why towards the end of this chapter.) Unfortunately, some researchers on gun control (Miller & Hemenway, 1999) have argued that the only acceptable evidence on gun control is randomized control trials. We take a more eclectic view. We support diverse scientific research (Leenaars, 2005; 2007); this is sometimes called the *"evidence-pyramid" model*, supported by the World Health Organization (WHO) (Tugwell & Knotternus, 2015). To support an open-minded view, we quote Tugwell and Knottnerus (2015): "Taking an evidence-based approach does not mean relying on or privileging only one kind of method, such as randomized control trial. It does not mean that there is only one hierarchy of evidence, and it does not mean an epistemological rejection of subjective positions or methods" (p. 1247).

Furthermore, on a different note, but equally relevant to an environmental control tactic, the research at the individual level showed the association of guns and suicide is not simplistic; there are a host of relevant factors. Psychopathology and drug/alcohol abuse, especially alcohol, for examples, are associated in the equation (Miller & Hemenway, 1999). If a suicidal person, for example, has a mental disorder, the presence of a gun in that home greatly increases the risk for suicide. Whether this is true in Canada, we do not know.

## Population Level Studies on Guns and Suicide: Gun Control Laws in Canada

Canada has a long history of firearm restrictions, unlike the USA. The first governmental act of gun control was issued in 1885. It was a police effort. It required gun control provisions in what are now the Northwest Territories, Nunavut, the Yukon, Alberta, Saskatchewan, and parts of Manitoba. It required permission from the government to own a firearm or ammunition. In 1892, under the then enacted Criminal Act, individuals needed a permit to carry a pistol, unless there was deemed threat or personal danger. In the 1920's, all non-citizens needed a permit to acquire a gun. Legislation in 1934 mandated that all handguns be registered with the Royal Canadian Mounted Police (RCMP), local police and/or other justice agency.

This became known as Canada's first gun registry. In 1935, no guns could be sold to people sixteen and under. In 1951, automatic firearms were added to the registry, and the gun registry became controlled by the RCMP. In 1969, Bill C-150 was enacted to categorize "Restricted", "Non-restricted", and "Prohibited". Despite these early efforts at firearm controls, there are no reliable data that can show whether any of these efforts worked. Science, thus, cannot help; yet, this fact never stopped many claiming, including the police, that they worked. It was only after a 1977 bill that science could shed light on what works!

An opportunity for studying the effects of legislative means restriction, e.g., gun control laws, on their use for suicide is provided by Canada's Criminal Law Amendment Act of 1977 (Bill C-51), enforced since 1978. This Act required acquisition certification for all firearms (FACs), restricted the availability of some types of firearms to certain types of individuals, set up procedures for handling and storing firearms, required permits for those selling firearms, introduced controls on the selling of ammunition, and increased the sentences for firearm offenses. People, including Canadian citizens, also needed to pass a basic criminal background check.

Early commentators on the impact of this Act (Mundt, 1990), reported little impact of the Act on firearm suicide in Canada, but the work was too simplistic. Mundt presented only simple charts, with no statistical analysis of the trends. He also studied only a few years, too few for statistical analysis. Lester and Leenaars (1993, 1994) reported the *first* comprehensive study on the preventive effect of the Act on suicide in Canada. They used appropriate statistical techniques and showed that one must have at least 7 years before and after the year that the law came into effect to show a significant or non-significant impact. Their results suggested that strict firearm control laws might well have been associated with changes in suicide rates due to the reduced use of firearms for suicide, and no overall switching from firearms to other methods for suicide. Lester and Leenaars' results suggest that Bill C-51 in Canada appeared to have had a significant positive impact, namely, lowering the rate of suicide by guns.

**Table 2. Suicide rates in Canada before and after passage of C-51**

| Year | Total | Suicide Rate | | % suicides by firearms |
|---|---|---|---|---|
| | | Firearms | Other Methods | |
| 1969 | 10.91 | 3.57 | 7.34 | 32.7 |
| 1970 | 11.33 | 3.74 | 7.59 | 33.0 |
| 1971 | 11.86 | 4.28 | 7.58 | 36.1 |
| 1972 | 12.19 | 4.29 | 7.90 | 35.2 |
| 1973 | 12.58 | 4.31 | 8.27 | 34.3 |
| 1974 | 12.98 | 4.57 | 8.41 | 35.2 |
| 1975 | 12.37 | 4.64 | 7.73 | 37.5 |
| 1976 | 12.76 | 4.76 | 8.00 | 37.3 |
| mean | 12.12 | 4.27 | 7.85 | 35.2 |
| sd | 0.72 | 0.42 | 0.36 | 1.8 |
| b | 0.26** | 0.16*** | 0.10 | 0.61** |
| 1977 | 14.26 | 5.46 | 8.80 | 38.3 |
| 1978 | 14.80 | 5.48 | 9.32 | 37.0 |
| 1979 | 14.18 | 4.65 | 9.53 | 32.8 |
| 1980 | 14.03 | 4.68 | 9.35 | 33.4 |
| 1981 | 13.98 | 4.81 | 9.17 | 34.4 |
| 1982 | 14.30 | 4.88 | 9.42 | 34.1 |
| 1983 | 15.09 | 4.97 | 10.12 | 33.0 |
| 1984 | 13.69 | 4.19 | 9.50 | 30.6 |
| 1985 | 12.85 | 4.10 | 8.75 | 31.9 |
| mean | 14.11 | 4.72 | 9.40 | 33.4 |
| sd | 0.68 | 0.44 | 0.38 | 1.9 |
| b | - 0.15 | - 0.13* | - 0.02 | - 0.57* |
| $t_{14}$ | 5.70** | 2.09* | 4.81** | 1.91* |

* one-tailed $p < .05$.

** one-tailed $p < .01$.

Rates are incidence per 100,000.

Subsequently, Leenaars and Lester (1997a) examined whether the restriction of firearms in Bill C-51 in Canada had a preventive impact for those of all ages or only for some ages. The results showed that the percentage of suicides using firearms decreased only for those aged 15-64, while it increased for those aged 65+. The data and results on suicide rates prior to and after the passage of Bill C-51 are presented in Table 2. It can be seen in Table 2 that the firearm suicide rate of the total population increased after the passage of the Act, from 4.27 per 100,000 per year to 4.72; the suicide rate by all other methods increased also, from 7.85 to 9.40. However, the percentage of suicides using firearms decreased after passage of the Act, from 35.2% to 33.4%. Furthermore, whereas prior to the passage of the Act, the firearm suicide rate was increasing (the slope of the regression line was 0.16), after passage of the Act the firearm suicide rate began to decrease (the slope of the regression line was - 0.13).

**Table 3. Changes in suicide rates from 1969-1976 to 1978-1985 by Ages**

| Age | Total | Rates | Other Methods | % by Firearms |
|---|---|---|---|---|
| | | Suicide Rate | | |
| 15-24: | | | | |
| 1969-1976: mean | 12.57 | 5.89 | 6.68 | 46.5 |
| 1978-1985: mean | 16.11[a] | 7.12[c] | 9.00[a] | 44.1 |
| 25-34: | | | | |
| 1969-1976: mean | 15.42 | 5.59 | 9.83 | 36.1 |
| 1978-1985: mean | 18.48[c] | 6.11 | 12.36[c] | 32.9[a] |
| 35-44: | | | | |
| 1969-1976: mean | 18.69 | 6.22 | 12.47 | 33.3 |
| 1978-1985: mean | 18.04 | 5.53[a] | 12.51 | 30.6[a] |
| 45-54: | | | | |
| 1969-1976: mean | 21.56 | 6.69 | 14.86 | 31.3 |
| 1978-1985: mean | 20.62 | 6.19[a] | 14.42 | 30.0 |
| 55-64: | | | | |
| 1969-1976: mean | 20.85 | 6.58 | 14.27 | 31.6 |
| 1978-1985: mean | 19.00 | 5.67[a] | 14.23 | 28.6[a] |
| 65-74: | | | | |
| 1969-1976: mean | 17.32 | 4.85 | 12.46 | 28.0 |
| 1978-1985: mean | 17.79 | 5.03 | 12.75 | 28.3 |
| 75+: | | | | |
| 1969-1976: mean | 12.91 | 3.34 | 9.58 | 25.7 |
| 1978-1985: mean | 15.51[b] | 4.54[b] | 10.97[a] | 29.0[a] |

[a] significantly different from the 1969-1976 mean $p < .05$.

[b] significantly different from the 1969-1976 mean $p < .01$.

[c] significantly different from the 1969-1976 mean $p < .001$.

Rates are incidence per 100,000.

The effects of passage of the Act as a function of the age of the suicide are shown in Table 3. Table 4 shows the linear trends. It can be seen that the firearm suicide rate decreased after passage of the Act only for suicides aged 35-64, whereas the firearm suicide rate increased for those aged 15-34 and 64+. The percentage of suicides using firearms decreased only for those aged 15-64, while it increased for those aged 65+. The conclusion seems to be that the impact on suicide of gun control laws in Canada was not evident in older adults.

As noted, the general conclusion seems to be that the impact on suicide of making gun control laws stricter in Canada was not apparent in those over the age of 65, but there was a significant impact on the young. Shneidman and Farberow (1957) showed that the suicidal elderly have a stronger intent to die than younger adults. They are less ambivalent and there is a chronic course (Leenaars, 2004). Younger suicides are more situationally disturbed and impulsive (Leenaars, 2004). Perhaps the (younger) individual may be sufficiently delayed by increased difficulty in obtaining the preferred method for suicide so that the suicidal pain has passed by the time that he or she has succeeded in obtaining the means for suicide. This would argue for waiting periods for the purchase of a firearm. The lack of impact on the elderly is consistent with other research (Lester, 1992) that, not only gun control, but also education programs, crisis intervention services, telephone crisis centers are less effective with the elderly than with younger adults. Thus, much more thought must be given, and research undertaken, to devising tactics for preventing suicide in the elderly (Richman, 1993).

There is evidence that men and women may respond differently to restricted access to lethal methods for suicide. A study by Leenaars and Lester (1996) was designed, therefore, to explore whether the 1977 gun control law in Canada had different effects for men and women in their use of guns for suicide. The results indicated that the passage of C-51 seemed to have had a greater impact on women than men in the use of firearms as a method for suicide, as some men may have switched method; this phenomenon is called *displacement*.

**Table 4. Linear trends in suicide rates from 1969-1976 to 1978-1985 by Ages (b coefficients shown)**

| Age | Total | Rates Firearms | Other Methods | % by Firearms |
|---|---|---|---|---|
| Suicide Rate | | | | |
| 15-24: | | | | |
| 1969-1976 | $0.77^{***}$ | $0.48^{*}$ | $0.29^{**}$ | $1.06^{**}$ |
| 1978-1985 | - 0.21 | $-0.25^{*}$ | 0.03 | - 0.95 |
| 25-34: | | | | |
| 1969-1976 | $0.53^{**}$ | $0.32^{**}$ | 0.20 | $0.85^{*}$ |
| 1978-1985 | - 0.29 | $-0.33^{*}$ | 0.03 | $-1.24^{**}$ |
| 35-44: | | | | |
| 1969-1976 | - 0.01 | 0.05 | - 0.06 | 0.28 |
| 1978-1985 | - 0.34 | $-0.32^{*}$ | - 0.02 | $-1.16^{*}$ |
| 45-54: | | | | |
| 1969-1976 | - 0.19 | - 0.09 | - 0.10 | - 0.11 |
| 1978-1985 | $-0.46^{*}$ | - 0.12 | $-0.34^{**}$ | 0.07 |
| 55-64: | | | | |
| 1969-1976 | - 0.57 | - 0.13 | - 0.45 | 0.26 |
| 1978-1985 | - 0.35 | - 0.01 | - 0.35 | 0.56 |
| 65-74: | | | | |
| 1969-1976 | - 0.04 | - 0.01 | - 0.03 | 0.03 |
| 1978-1985 | - 0.10 | 0.13 | - 0.23 | 0.92 |
| 75+: | | | | |
| 1969-1976 | $-0.33^{*}$ | - 0.12 | $-0.21^{**}$ | - 0.20 |
| 1978-1985 | 0.05 | 0.02 | 0.03 | 0.55 |

* $p < .05$.

** $p < .01$.

*** $p < .001$.

Rates are incidence per 100,000.

Carrington (1999) questioned the Leenaars and Lester (1996) data, suggesting that significant downward changes in death rates for suicide for both men and women occurred, with no evidence for switching method in both sexes, but he used a simple chi-square test. In response, Leenaars, Moksony, Lester, & Wenckstern (2003) re-evaluated, using complex interrupted time-series analysis, and supported the findings of Leenaars and Lester. They found that, although the intervention had an impact on both men and women, the impact was stronger and more enduring in women. Although there was an impact on men, probably because many more men than women use firearms, a significant percentage of men showed displacement. Displacement was not observed in a significant percentage of women. Thus, public health approaches, such as gun control, may have limits in interventions. Females show the stronger impact of gun control on homicide too (Leenaars & Lester, 1996); the reasons are diverse. For example, men, of course, show a greater use of lethal means (WHO, 2002); firearms are often a preferred method for suicide. Suicidal women show a greater response to clinical intervention programs, educational endeavours, use of telephone crisis centers, and receiving care for psychiatric disturbances (Lester, 1995). Thus, it makes sense that this would be true with tactics of environmental control; it is almost a 'universal' accepted fact that women are more positively affected by intervention(s). This would suggest a strong push for more gender specific research in *prevention*. Yet, research to explore the phenomenon and to develop gender-specific interventions is lacking.

Stack (1998), in a review of gun control studies, pointed out that rarely do gun control studies take into account other societal factors (confounders), which may influence the suicide rate, factors such as divorce, unemployment and the age structure of the population. A study by Leenaars, Moksony, Lester, and Wenckstern (2003) examined this critique of this public health strategy. In order to see whether social changes might have had an impact on suicide rates from guns, birth, marriage and divorce rates as measures of domestic integration (a social variable which Durkheim [1897] argued was critical in determining suicide rates), the unemployment rate (Platt, 1984), median family income and the percentage of the males aged 15 to 24 years as a percentage of the total male population (a group with one of Canada's highest suicide rates) were studied. The results showed that the passage of Bill C-51 in Canada in 1977, introducing stricter gun control, appears to have been followed by a significant reduction in the suicide rate by firearms, even after controlling for some social variables. Thus, it appears that, even if one controls for other social variables, gun control works.

There may, of course, have been social changes other than those considered that might be responsible for changes in the suicide rates, and the use of a different set of social indicators (such as drug use) might change the estimates of the impact of the passage of Bill C-51. However, data on such factors were not available. For example, alcohol and drug consumption data in Canada have only been available since 1985 (E. Simoneti, Statistics Canada, personal communication, August 19, 1999). Canada's Department of Justice (1996) has also isolated a few other social variables that may be associated with suicide in Canada, such as the percentage of foreign-born, and education levels, but data were not available. The role of these and other social factors should be studied in the future, if and when the necessary data become available.

Some researchers have disputed the conclusion that gun restriction has prevented suicide in Canada and elsewhere (Sloan, Rivera, Reay et al., 1990; Kassirer, 1991; Kleck, 1991; Rich, Young, Fowler et al., 1990). Be that as it may, Carrington and Moyer (1994a, 1994b) replicated the positive findings for gun control in Ontario and showed a similar pattern for most of Canada's provinces and that all provinces had either stable or decreasing rates of firearm suicides, following C-51. Results on related phenomena of homicide (Leenaars & Lester, 2001) and accidental deaths (Leenaars & Lester, 1997b) hold equal promise.

There have been two subsequent laws to increase gun control in Canada, Bill C-17 and C-68. In 1991, Bill C-17, the Conservative (like Republicans in the USA) government's bill, tightened the screening provisions for firearm acquisition (FAC). (We note here that this was a Conservative bill because it was/is wrongly assumed by many that only the left leaning parties [Liberals and New Democratic Party, the former similar to USA Democrats] implemented gun control laws in Canada.) It required the FAC applicant to pass a safety course. It mandated very strict background checks, a more complete search of an applicant's personal and criminal records, and a 28-day waiting period. It introduced tighter control of military and paramilitary guns and prohibited high-capacity ammunition for automatic and semi-automatic firearms. It also limited handguns more. It more clearly defined what was meant by firearms storage, handling, and transportation. Bill C-17 also increased penalties for firearm crimes.

Like Bill C-51, there are reliable data in Canada to study the impact of this Act. Bridges (2004), following Leenaars and Lester's design, examined the impact of the Act and showed a significant decrease after passage of Bill C-17 in the rate of suicides involving firearms and the percentage of suicides (and homicides) using firearms. Bridges examined the use of firearms for suicide during the 7-year period prior (1984-1990) to the bill and the 7 years (1991-1998) after the passing of Bill C-17 to measure the association of the bill with rates of suicide by method. The rate of suicide by firearms (from means of 4.09 per 100,000 per year to 3.17) and the percentage of suicides using firearms (from 31.2% to 24.5%) decreased significantly. Be that as it may, people may have switched method; the rate of suicide by other methods increased (from 9.02 to 9.76). However, statistical analysis (linear regression) revealed that there were no significant changes in the total rate of suicide and the rate of suicide by other methods. Bridges concluded that "If persons did switch from using firearms to other methods for suicide, this tendency did not significantly increase from 1992 to 1998" (p 822-823). Thus, we may conclude that there may not have been significant displacement after the bill.

Gagné, Robitaille, Hamel, and St-Laurent (2010) have also reported that, in the province of Quebec, firearm regulations were associated with declining rates of male suicides. However, Caron (2004) in a study of a specific region in Northern Quebec (Abitibi-Témiscaminque, the region in Quebec with the highest suicide rate and highest firearm suicide rate) found no evidence of an overall impact on the suicide rate for males in general and males over 45. There was a downward trend in women. Furthermore, there was a noticeable decrease in firearm suicide in the under-25 age group (the age group with the highest increase in suicide). However, the youth may have switched to hanging, as there was an increase in suicide by hanging, resulting in no overall significant change in the rate of suicide in that age group. Caron, Julien and Huang (2008) analyzed the impact of the same law in Quebec and suggested evidence for the substitution hypothesis in which firearm suicide may have been replaced by hanging among males. Cheung and Dewa (2005) examined the possibility of switching after the bill in youth between 15-19 years of age in Canada. They studied the age-specific suicide rates for youth between 1979 and 1999 and found that the overall rates of suicide did not change over this same time period. On a different point, these studies raise questions on age specific impacts of gun control.

In 1995, Bill C-68 was introduced and amended the Criminal Code. It implemented a new central licensing system to replace the FAC procedure. Bill C-68 clearly spelled out specific restrictions of banned short-barreled and small caliber handguns. It also required the registration of all guns and gun license owners. It required a license to buy ammunition. There was, however, a provision for "grandfathering" previous owners of some firearms. Like Bill C-17 and Bill-C-51, there are *some* data to study this Act; however, there are serious reliability problems in the data.

Bill C-68 was viewed by some as more an attempt at people control, than gun control. It required people to register all shotguns and rifles. It was to be implemented in 1999, then 2001, then in 2003, and then finally in 2006. In 2001 the registry bill was to be implemented, but the government simply asked people to freely register their guns. In 2003, it became mandatory; failure to do so resulted in a violation of criminal law. Yet, in 2006, although the law was still in place, it temporarily protected licensed owners of non-restricted guns (even if the license had expired by January 1, 2004). Bill C-68 continued to have mounting problems and was, in fact, never fully enacted. On October 25, 2011, the Conservative government introduced a bill to amend the Criminal Code and the Firearms Act, to abolish long-gun registry and destroy all records. On February 15, 2012, Bill C-19 was passed and became law, which ended any possibility of studying Bill C-68.

From a research perspective alone, Bill C-68 had mounting problems for study; indeed, Bill C-68 was never empirically studied and can never be reliably studied. For example, as Leenaars and Lester (1997a) showed, at least seven post-years of a bill is needed to reliably make a conclusion of the impact. Basically stated, what would be the independent variable or more accurately, predictive variable? What date? Time-line? Can we even use

2006 to begin the study? The answer: No! (This was a problem in early studies, such as Mundt's in Canada.) The Bill itself, unlike C-17, for example, was quite controversial in Canada; there was significant opposition. Unlike the former laws, there was opposition and non-compliance by diverse groups such as Indigenous people, farmers, gun lobbyists, and hunters. The Conservative government, in fact, introduced Bill C-19 to rescind the registry in response to these voices. There was a great deal of political debate, but little research presented, only values and beliefs. This does not mean that values and beliefs are not important, only that there was a great deal of sensational coverage, but *no* research. We should base our decisions about "Does it work?" on evidence-informed facts. In fact, research was rarely discussed in Canada's national papers or news, only the polemics about the registry. Of course, this is quite normal around the world. Facts do not make laws; often only false facts do. (False information is known to travel faster and more quantitatively than truth.)

A police report, *RCMP Canadian Firearms Program*, was released in February 2010 and concluded that the gun registry did work. Regrettably, the police dissembled the data in the report (Leenaars, 2100). The report regressed information to the days of Mundt. It presented only simple charts and tables, and no statistical analysis (which is, of course, not possible anyway, given that we need at least 7 years of data after the year the law came into effect). Mundt, we assume, would be pleased. Of course, the RCMP has been in charge (control) of gun control in Canada for over a hundred years, not the people. From a researcher's point of view, the bill can never be studied. There are further non-empirical questions about the effectiveness of strict shotgun and rifle registration. Farmers, hunters, Indigenous people and many other people in Canada, like elsewhere around the world on this issue, have been defiant, maybe understandably. They viewed this act as a control of their common rights, which they always had in Canada. Regrettably, there was extremism on both sides of the debate, both the rifle associations and the anti-gun coalition. The anti-gun proponents were, in fact, not science (evidence) based; they only showed distorted logic, such as jumping to conclusions and magnification.

A cognitive-behavioral (CBT) psychotherapist would label it, irrational and faulty beliefs. This does not help our search for answers. Indeed, the false claims and politicking by the gun control group (such as Canada's Coalition for Gun Control) bear some responsibility for the defeat of Bill C-68. The pro-rifle associations in Canada were no different, however. Newspapers typically only covered the sensational. As the Canadian philosopher, Marshall McLuhan, noted, the medium is the message; more people control. A thought experiment: Imagine if Canadians knew the answers to the following questions, "What is the problem?", and "What are the cause(s), patterns, and associations of the problem?" The Canadian people need to know the facts about suicide prevention (and for that matter, accident and homicide prevention too), and thus, we think then, they and maybe the politicians too can make informed decisions on means restriction. Environmental controls, at least within public health, are known to be more effective than people controls. Simply stated, not all controls are accepted, and that has huge implications in the effectiveness of an intervention. This debate in Canada, of course, is not unusual about gun control worldwide (Leenaars, 2006). To conclude: gun registration did not work in Canada! Not because we have studies, but because of the polemics!

However, before we assume that registration absolutely does *not* work, we want to point to a study in Norway. Gjertsen, Leenaars, and Vollrath (2014) studied the effect of four firearm restrictions on firearm deaths in Norway between 1969 and 2009. All deaths due to firearm discharge (5,660 deaths, both sexes) were examined. Yet, the data limitations, such as few female cases, allowed only study of males. The total deaths revealed that 89% of firearm deaths (both sexes) were suicides, 8% were homicides, and 3% were accidental. Gjertson et al. found that a 1991 regulation, requiring a police permit before acquiring a shotgun, had a positive impact on suicide in the total sample and in those aged 15-34. Interestingly, Gjertson et al. showed that only gun registry worked to reduce suicide, not other laws. Maybe, we are still left with the question, "Does gun registry work?"

## Population Level Studies: Gun Control in Other Countries

More research is needed, however, to strengthen the conclusion that the passage of gun control laws in Canada works. We need to look beyond Canada. There is research, of course, elsewhere. For example, Beautrais, Fergusson and Horwood (2006) examined the impact of more restrictive firearm legislation (Amendment to the Arms Act, 1992) in New Zealand on suicides involving firearms. The amendment restricted accessibility, required confidentiality checks of two references, and introduced more strict storage and safety requests. After the legislation, it was shown that firearm-related suicide decreased dramatically, especially in youth. Thus, the New Zealand study not only replicated some of the Canadian findings, but also supported the finding that the tactic was especially useful with young people, a high-risk group for suicide globally.

In the last 30 years or so, the positive effects of gun control laws have also been studied in the USA and Australia. These studies also support the research of Leenaars and Lester, the most comprehensive studies to date on any continent (see Lester, 2000). For example, in the USA, Ludwig and Cook (2000), Maxwell, Stolensky, Goodman, et al. (1984), Medoff and Magaddino (1983) and Sommers (1984) have reported that gun controls work. The various studies also offered some data on the fact that these impacts were true even if one controls for some social factors. The number of factors that were studied, however, was few. This warrants caution in overgeneralizing, something Leenaars and his colleagues (2003) attempted to rectify. Most important, restriction of sales of firearms to some people, such as people with mental disorders (psychopathology), may be important. This was also noted at the individual level of analysis. One, in fact, must control for psychopathology in environmental control tactics, both at an individual and societal level. Yet, further studies need to explore what is effective not only at an individual level but also at national and international levels. The science of controlling the environment for means is at that stage of study now. Probably regional, national and cultural differences will emerge. For example, the USA is known to be an outlier, even among developed, industrialized nations in firearm violence (Hahn, Bilukha, Crosby, et al., 2003), never mind other countries. (See Hahn et al., 2003 for the Centers for Disease Control and Prevention [CDC] review of USA firearm laws, not only for suicide but related violent phenomena, such as homicide.)

In Australia, as an example from that country, after a 1996 firearm massacre in Tasmania in which 35 people died, the Australian government undertook gun law reforms. Legislation restricted the sale of semi-automatic shotguns and rifles to civilians. It also legislated gun registration, prohibited private sales, and required dealers to be licensed. Chapman, Alpers, Aglo and Jones (2006), using official statistics, showed that after the law was enacted there was an accelerated decline in firearm deaths, especially suicides. This Australian example once more shows that removing lethal means in the environment could be associated with a sudden and ongoing reduction in suicides and related phenomena of homicide and accidental deaths. This finding is consistent at both the individual and population levels of analysis.

## CONCLUSION 1: SOME LESSONS FROM CANADA

There are numerous studies on the impact of guns on suicide, such as firearm ownership, availability of guns in the home and firearm storage (see Lester, 2000; Leenaars, 2007; Miller & Hemenway, 1999 for reviews). Studies on the availability of guns show that, if guns are present, then the rate of use for the means of suicide increases. Individual level studies, mainly in the USA, show that the more guns in the home, the more suicides, especially in the young. However, none of these studies were undertaken in Canada. Be that as it may, population level studies in Canada show the same patterns and associations. There are consistencies (commonalities) in the empirical studies, both individual and ecological. Most of the empirical studies, together with gun control law studies across the globe, show that availability of a potentially dangerous means affects the rate of use of the means for death (WHO, 2006). (We would encourage a consultation of the 2006 WHO document, *Preventing disease through healthy environments*.)

There are arguments against the impact of gun control, of course. Kleck, an NRA supporter has been the most vocal in that point of view. Kleck (1991, 1997) has argued that researchers on the topic of gun control have used illegitimate analyses, offered false conclusions, and so on. Gun control does *not* work! Kleck (1991, 1997; Britt, Bondua & Kleck, 1996) presented his own data and analysis to show that gun control fails to reduce the rate of suicide and violence in general. Yet, Hemenway (1999) and others have pointed out, not only the problems in Kleck's analysis, but also Kleck's use of questionable, inconsistent, and misleading statistics. Although Kleck, the NRA, and many other pro-gun scientists, do not seem to know (or wish to know) that one cannot accept the null hypothesis in science; this has not stopped them from making such *false* facts. Hypothesis testing has been misused and misinterpreted. Hemenway (2009) points out when you find nothing, it does *not* mean that "THERE WAS NO EFFECT" (p. 266; bold capital letters by Hemenway). The fact that there may be a lack of evidence does not mean that we can accept the null hypothesis; yet, researchers like Kleck jump to conclusions from poorly designed, limited studies that the null hypothesis is true. Hemenway (2009) points out that that conclusion is far too strong (i.e., magnification). He writes:

> In statistics, as in life, it is always possible to find what one is supposedly looking for, or in other words, to find nothing. There are various reasons, including not having the right tools (for example, enough data), not looking in the right place, and not being particularly interested in finding something. Another reason is that there is nothing to be found. However, when one does not undertake good search, finding nothing does not mean very much. (p. 265)

Regrettably, this was true for Mundt in Canada, and has been true of some studies, such as Kleck's, in the USA. Studies do not even have to be poorly designed and poorly executed. Researchers should know better, even if the public, media, and NRA do not. Of course, this is not only true about suicide, but also homicide. For example, Langmann (2012) studied firearm homicides in Canada from 1947 to 2008 and reported relatively few effects from the legislative changes and concluded firearms legislation does *not* work!

Cummings et al. (1997), at an individual level, and Leenaars et al. (2003), at a population level, have also introduced complex statistical analyses and controls for possible confounders to the field, ones that address Kleck's arguments about statistics and designs in the field. With such controls in the research, the associations between the availability of guns and suicide hold. The disagreements, of course, continue and Leenaars (2006) has predicted that they will increase internationally to polemic levels. This prediction has been shown to be true!

In public health policy, legislation is used as a means to control the environment and improve safety and health, such as reducing suicide and other firearm deaths and injuries (Chapman, 2001; Gjertsen, Leenaars, Vollrath, 2014; Hahn et al., 2003; Leenaars, 2007; Leenaars et al., 2000; WHO, 2002). However, assessing and quantifying the possible impact of a new law is a challenge. While that may be true, it should challenge us to research-action.

The tactic of controlling the environment is more complex than gun control, although it is a prototypical example. Referring to gun control as a means for suicide prevention in Canada and in the USA probably makes sense because it is those countries' main method of suicide (although there are exceptions in Canada and USA, such as Indigenous people for whom hanging is the main method). The gun is a highly lethal method. However, in other countries, guns are not a frequent means. For example, in Cuba, firearms are the least frequent means for committing suicide in the nation. Hanging, immolation, poisoning by insecticides/pesticides, and drowning are common methods in different countries. There is social acceptability for particular methods of dying by suicide. However, suicide by firearms is increasing in many nations. For example, hanging is the most common method in Thailand, but the use of firearms is increasing. Firearm suicides have increased in Russia. The same is true in Colombia, the world's most violent country (WHO, 2002). Thus, one can see great variation in means and, although gun control may make little sense in some regions of the five continents, the tactic of controlling the environment may well have increasing applicability, as suggested in the WHO report (Bertolote, 1993), and as studies show on different continents (Leenaars, Cantor, Connolly et al., 2002). The research, both at the individual level and population level of analysis, is perhaps unequivocal on the question, "What works?": Availability of firearms increases the risk of suicide and restriction of firearms decreases the risk of suicide (at least in Canada).

## CONCLUSION 2: DO THE LESSONS IN CANADA MEAN ANYTHING FOR THE UNITED STATES?

One cannot cease from exploration (or questioning). Of course, *a priori*, it is obvious that this volume is an American book. Therefore, it seems natural to ask, "Do Canada's studies apply to the USA?" "Does the gun control that works in Canada, work in the USA?" ("And elsewhere around the world?") We do not know. Science will be the answer, provided we utilize an "evidence-pyramid" model. Although there have been some early studies on the question (Leenaars, 1995), more study is needed. Cross-cultural study is the next big need in gun control, and for that matter, suicidology in general. The concept (theory) of firearms control, in Canada and the USA, we believe, must follow Seymore Lipset's (1990) frame (map) of the continental divide. What does that mean? To answer, we begin with a quote from a Canadian icon, Margaret Atwood (1972), in her analysis of American-Canadian literature differences:

> "In American literature the family is something the hero must repudiate and leave; it is the structure he rebels against, thereby defining his own freedom ... In Canadian literature the family is handled quite differently ... in Canada it's a trap in which you're caught ... he feels the need to escape, but somehow he is unable to break away" (p. 131).

Elsewhere, Atwood (1972) notes that, unlike Canada, the United States "holds out hope, never fulfilled but always promised, of a Utopia, the perfect human society" (p. 31-32).

What we know (Leenaars, 1995: Leenaars, Wenckstern, Sakinofsky et al., 1998): For decades the rates of suicide among Canadians have been higher (but that reversed consistently around 2010). Since the early 1970s, Canada had a higher rate of suicide than the USA. Canadian youth had higher rates of suicide (but American youth kill others much more, as does the general population) (See Table 1 above). In the 15-19 age-group, Canada's youth suicide rate was for decades at 50 to 60% higher. Thus, if we take the USA rate as 100%, then the Canadian youth suicide rate was at 160%. This trend reversed around 2010, and the USA now has higher rates in youth suicide and homicide. Why? Of course, it is true that Americans have always had a very significantly higher rate of homicide, about 400% higher, and this is true in youth. The American rate is around 400% to 500% higher. (One can make all sorts of speculations about historical and even current gun availability.) Attitudes towards suicide differ greatly; Canadians accept suicide more as a normal solution to unbearable pain, psychache or suffering. Canadians believe more in suicide myths, or said alternatively, in false suicide facts. Religion and values help Americans more as protective factors. Gun control is more accepted in Canada. Gun control has been shown to be effective (well, sometimes) in Canada; maybe not so in the USA.

Andrew Malcolm (1988) concluded that "adversity is instinctively anticipated in Canada, an attitude that has produced a kind of self-fulfilling pessimism" (p. 1). Guns solve that problem. Guns are an effective solution for the barren pain. Gun control was more accepted, almost without protest. Police (RCMP) controlled the nation and still try to do so. Americans rebelled against control; Canadians have opposed little (Bill C-19 is a good example of the exception). S.D. Clark's (1962) speculation may well best account for Canadian and American values and behavior where suicide and gun control are concerned.

Max Weber (1949), a father of modern sociology, was one of the first to provide the speculation that to understand current events, one had to search the history. (Among other reasons, Weber is famous for his insightful methodology essays, written between 1903 and 1917. They were translated and edited by Edward Shils and Henry Finch in 1949 in *The methodology of the social sciences.*) Weber especially argued that we need to look at societal, cultural, governmental, and environmental levels within the WHO ecological model. Historical events, Weber showed, help explain current differences, and this is very true about the USA and Canada. There are very significant and radically different histories in the USA and Canada; this is very true about firearm histories. (We earlier briefly outlined Canada's, and the reader can find ample documentation on the USA in this volume.) Weber argued by analogy that as one rolls a dice (i.e., a decision) a certain number (that same decision) becomes more likely to be repeated. A decision in Canada reinforces that same decision; say the long history of ever increasing gun controls, to the point of taking "grandfather's" prized 1800's shotgun away. Another decision in the United States reinforces that decision, such as the Second Amendment, the right to bear arms, in the American Constitution. Here, Weber argued, both countries' histories reinforce their values and behaviors – for example, on gun control. Lipset (1990) notes:

> My central argument is that the two countries differ in their basic organizing principles. Canada has been and is more class aware, elitist, law-abiding, statest, collective oriented, and particularist (group-oriented) society than the United States. These fundamental distinctions stem in large part from the American Revolution and the diverse social and environmental ecologies flowing from the division of British North America. The social effects of this separation were then reinforced by variation in literature, religious traditions, political and legal institutions, and socio-economic structures. (p. 8)

The foremost Canadian scholar in the area is S.D. Clark (1962; Hiller, 1982). Clark (1962) notes: "Whereas the American nation was a product of the revolutionary spirit, the Canadian nation grew mainly out of forces of a counter-revolution" (p. 190-191). He speculated that differences between Canada and the United States can best be explained by their history, how people in these countries settled their respective frontiers. Canadians moved westward under the organization of the British Government, the influence of the military police, and the favor of the two predominant churches (the Church of England and the Roman Catholic Church). In contrast, America's frontier was settled independently, not as an "outpost of the empire." Canada remained loyal to Britain; the United States was established as a revolution against Britain. The revolutionary attitude in the United States is distinct from the more conservative attitude in Canada. It is this explanation, according to Clark and others (e.g., Lipset), that best accounts for the divergence in the two nations. This is true about gun control! It 'threw the dice' to develop the continental divide. We believe this difference is true in gun control, not only the history but in the implications and applications. Our studies show that gun control often works in Canada; the history shows why, and maybe why there is more rebellion towards gun control in the USA, and therefore, why it may be less effective, even to try to control guns in the USA.

Margaret Atwood (1972), one of Canada's best-known authors today, suggests that the symbol for the United States is "the Frontier . . . a place that is *new*, where the old can be discarded." The American Revolution divided the new from the old. In contrast, in Canada the symbol is "Survival", a place where one is "hanging on, staying alive". Canadians hang on to Britain. A quote from her intriguing book, *Survival* (1972), is most revealing, especially in its direct application to suicide. She notes:

> Canadians are forever taking the national pulse …. Our central idea is one which generates, not the excitement and sense of adventure or danger which The Frontier holds out, not the smugness and/or sense of security, of everything in its place .... but an almost intolerable anxiety. (p. 33)

Analyses of art, history, politics, religion, psychology, violence, suicide, homicide, etc. and *gun control* lead to the same conclusion: There is a continental divide!

To put our historical dig into a nutshell: In Canada, it would be, "Gun control by the police (RCMP)"; whereas, in the USA, it would be, "Anti-gun control by the NRA." This is a huge difference, a continental divide. (P.S: From a CBT view, putting things in a nutshell is 'distorted thinking'.)

In our chapter, we think the best way to understand the answer to our last question is the cultural approach that accounts for Canadian-American differences in suicide (and violence) and gun control. All knowledge, as Weber noted, is cultural reality. This is consistent with the WHO's (2002) *ecological* model. Atwood, Clark, Leenaars, Lipset, Weber, and others have all expounded this view. Others (see Lipset, 1990) have proposed a convergence theory; yet, in firearms control, we see no evidence, only greater differences in gun control on the continent. Therefore, we do not think the Canadian studies absolutely apply to the USA; maybe they work in the USA, but maybe not. All that we know is that gun control works in Canada, but that the effect (or impact) of gun control is complex rather than simple. Finally, of course, there is no *absolute* objective verified scientific fact of the efficacy of gun control. That is true, however, about all scientific facts.

## REFERENCES

Adjacic-Gross, V., Killias, M, Hepp, U., Gadola, E., Bapp, M., Lauber, C., Schnyder, U., Gutzwiller, F. & Rössler, W. (2006). Changing times: A longitudinal analysis of international firearm suicide data. *American Journal of Public Health*, *96*, 1752-1755.

Atwood, M. (1972). *Survival.* Toronto, ON: Anansi.

Ayer, A. (Ed.) (1959). *Logical Positivism.* New York: NY: Free Press.

Bailey, J., Kellerman, A., Somes, G., Banton, J., Rivara, F. & Rushforth, N. (1997). Risk factors for violent death of women in the home. *Archives of Internal Medicine*, *157*, 777-782.

Beautrais, A., Fergusson, D. & Horwood, L. (2006). Firearms legislation and reduction in firearms-related suicide deaths in New Zealand. *Australian and New Zealand Journal of Psychiatry*, *40*, 253- 259.

Beautrais, A., Joyce, P. & Mulder, R. (1996). Access to firearms and the risk of suicide. *Australian & New Zealand Journal of Psychiatry*, *30*, 741-748.

Bertolote, J. (Ed.). (1993). *Guidelines for the primary prevention of mental, neurological and psychosocial disorders: Suicide.* Geneva, Switzerland: World Health Organization (WHO).

Brent, D., Perper, J., Allman, C., Moritz, G., Wartella, M. & Zelenak, J. (1991). The presence and accessibility of firearms in the homes of adolescent suicides. *Journal of the American Medical Association (JAMA)*, *266*, 2989-2995.

Brent, D., Perper, J., Goldstein, G., Kolko, D., Allan, M., Allman, C. & Zelenak, J. (1988). Risk factors for adolescent suicide. A comparison of adolescent suicide victims with suicidal inpatients. *Archvies of General Psychiatry*, *45*, 581-588.

Brent, D., Perper, J., Moritz, G., Baugher, M., Schweers, J. & Roth, C. (1993). Firearms and adolescent suicide. *American Journal of Diseases of Children*, *147*, 1066-1071.

Bridges, F. (2004). Gun control law (Bill C-17), suicide, and homicide in Canada. *Psychological Reports*, *94*, 819-826.

Britt, C., Bondua, D. & Kleck, G. (1996). A reassessment of the DC gun law: some cautionary notes on the use of interrupted time series designs for policy impact-assessment. *Law & Society Review*, *30*, 361-380.

Bronfenbrenner, U. (1979). *The ecology of human development: Experts by nature and design*. Cambridge, MA: Harvard University Press.

Caron, J. (2004). Gun control and suicide: Possible impact of Canadian legislation to ensure safe storage of firearms. *Archives of Suicide Research*, *8*, 195-208.

Caron, J., Julien, M. & Huang, J. (2008). Changes in suicide methods in Quebec between 1987 and 2000: The possible impact of Bill C-17 requiring safe storage of firearms. *Suicide and Life-Threatening Behavior*, *38*, 195-208.

Carrington, P. (1999). Gender, gun control, suicide and homicide in Canada *Archives of Suicide Research*, *5*, 71-75.

Carrington, P. & Moyer, S. (1994a). Gun control and suicide in Ontario. *American Journal of Psychiatry*, *151*, 606-608.

Carrington, P. & Moyer, S. (1994b). Gun availability and suicide in Canada. *Studies on Crime and Crime Prevention*, *3*, 168-178.

Chapman, S. (2001). Advocacy in public health: Roles and challenges. *International Journal of Epidemiology*, *30*, 1226-1232.

Chapman, S., Alpers, P., Aglo, K. & Jones, M. (2006). Australia's 1996 gun law reforms: Faster falls in firearm deaths, firearm suicides, and a decade with mass shootings. *Injury Prevention*, *12*, 365-372.

Cheung, A. & Dewa, C. (2005). Current trends in youth suicide and firearm regulation. *Canadian Journal of Public Health*, *96*, 131-135.

Clark, S. D. (1962). *The developing Canadian community.* Toronto, ON: University of Toronto Press.

Cummings, P., Koepsell, T., Grossman, D., Savarino, J. & Thompson, R. (1997). The association between the purchase of a handgun and homicide and suicide. *American Journal of Public Health*, *87*, 974-978.

Dahlberg, L. & Krug, E. (2002). Violence—A global public health problem. In WHO (Ed.), *World report on violence and health*, (pp. 1–21). Geneva, Switzerland: WHO.

Department of Justice, Canada. (1996). *A statistical analysis of the impacts of the 1977 firearms control legislation.* Ottawa: Department of Justice.

Durkheim, E. (1897). *Le suicide*. Paris: Felix Alcan.

Etzersdorfer, E., Kapusta, N. & Sonneck, G. (2006). Suicide by shooting is correlated to rate of gun licenses in Austrian counties. *Wiener Klinische Wochenschrift*, *118*, 464-468.

Gagné, M., Robitaille, Y., Hamel, D. & St-Laurent, D. (2010). Firearms regulation and declining rates of male suicides in Canada. *Injury Prevention*, *16*, 247-253.

Garbarino, J. & Crouter, A. (1978). Defining the community context for child-parent relations: The correlations of child maltreatment. *Child Development*, *49*, 604-616.

Gjertsen, F., Leenaars, A. & Vollrath, M. (2014). Mixed impact of firarms restrictions on fatal firearm injuries in males: a national observational study. *International Research of Environmental Research and Public Health*, *11*, 487-506.

Hahn, R., Bilukha, O., Crosby, A., Fullilove, M., Liberman, A., Moscicki, E., Snyder, S., Tuma, F. & Briss, P. (2003). First reports evaluating the effectiveness of strategies for preventing violence: Firearms laws. *MMWR. Morbidity and Mortality Weekly Report.*, Oct. 3, 2003, *52*, 11-20.

Hemenway, D. (1999). Risk & benefits of gun ownership. Letter, *Journal of the American Medical Association (JAMA)*, *282*, 135-136.

Hemenway, D. (2009). How to find nothing. *Journal of Public Health Policy*, *30*, 260-268.

Hiller, H. (1982). *Society and change: S.D. Clark and the development of Canadian sociology*. Toronto, ON: University of Toronto Press.

Jenkins, R. & Singh, B. (2000). General population strategies of suicide prevention. In K. Hawton & K. van Heeringen (Eds.), *The international handbook of suicide and attempted suicide*, (pp. 597-615). Chichester, UK: John Wiley & Sons.

Kassirer, J. (1991). Firearms and the killing threshold. *New England Journal of Medicine*, *325*, 1647-1650.

Kellerman, A., Rivara, F., Somes, G., Reay, D., Francisco, J., Banton, J., Prodzinski, J., Fligner, C. & Hackman, B. (1992). Suicide in the home in relation to gun ownership. *New England Journal of Medicine*, *327*, 467-472.

Killias, M. (1993). International correlations between gun ownership and rates of homicide and suicide. *Canadian Medical Association Journal*, *148*, 1721-1725.

Killias, M., Kesteren, J. & Rindisbacher, M. (2001). Guns, violent crime, and suicide in 21 countries. *Canadian Journal of Criminology*, *43*, 429-448.

Kleck, G. (1991). *Point blank*. New York: Aldine de Gruyter.

Kleck, G. (1997). *Targeting guns: Firearms and their control*. New York: Aldine de Gruyter.

Kreitman, N. (1976). The coal gas story. *British Journal of Preventive and Social Medicine*, *30*, 86-93.

Langmann, C. (2012). Canadian firearm legislation and effects on homicide 1974 to 2008. *Journal of Interpersonal Violence*, *27*, 2303-2321.

Leenaars, A. (1988). *Suicide notes*. New York, NY: Human Sciences.

Leenaars, A. (1995). Suicide and the Continental Divide. *Archives of Suicide Research*, *1*, 39-58.

Leenaars, A. (2004). *Psychotherapy with suicidal people*. Chichester, UK: John Wiley & Sons.

Leenaars, A. (2005). Effective public health strategies in suicide prevention are possible: A selective review of recent studies. *Clinical Neuropsychiatry*, *2*, 21-31.

Leenaars, A. (2006). Suicide by shooting and gun ownership (licenses) in Austria: Would gun restriction help? *Wiener Klinische Wochenschrift*, *118*, 439-441.

Leenaars, A. (2007). Gun-control legislation and the impact on suicide. *Crisis*, *28*, 50-57.

Leenaars, A. (2010). *Suicide and homicide-suicide among police.* London & New York: Routledge.

Leenaars, A., Cantor, C., Connolly, J., EchoHawk, M., Gailiene, D., He, Z., Kokorina, N., Lester, D., Lopatin, A., Rodriguez, M., Schlebusch, L., Takahashi, Y., Vijayakumar, L. & Wenckstern, S. (2000). Controlling the environment to prevent suicide: International perspectives. *Canadian Journal of Psychiatry*, *45*, 639- 644.

Leenaars, A., De Leo, D., Goldney, R., Gulbinat, W. & Wallace, D. (Eds.). (1998). The prevention of suicide: Controlling the environment. *Archives of Suicide Research*, *4*, 1-107.

Leenaars, A., Dieserud, G., Wenckstern, S., Dyregrov, K., Lester, D. & Lyke, J. (2018). A multidimensional theory of suicide: A psychological autopsy corroborative study. *Crisis*, *39*, xx-xx.

Leenaars, A. & Lester, D. (1996). Gender and the impact of gun control on suicide and homicide. *Archives of Suicide Research*, *2*, 223-234.

Leenaars, A. & Lester, D. (1997a). The impact of gun control on suicide and homicide across the life span. *Canadian Journal of Behavioural Science*, *29*, 1-6.

Leenaars, A. & Lester, D. (1997b). The effects of gun control on the accidental death rate from firearms in Canada. *Journal of Safety Research*, *28*, 119-122.

Leenaars, A. & Lester, D. (2001). The impact of gun control (Bill C-51) on homicide. *Journal of Criminal Justice*, *29*, 287-294.

Leenaars, L., Moksony, F., Lester, D. & Wenckstern, S. (2003). The impact of gun control (Bill C-51) on suicide in Canada. *Death Studies*, *27*, 103-124.

Leenaars, A. Wenckstern, S., Sakinofsky, I., Dyck, R., Kral, M. & Bland, R. (Eds.). *Suicide in Canada.* Toronto: ON; University of Toronto Press.

Lester, D. (1988a). Gun control, gun ownership and suicide prevention. *Suicide & Life-Threatening Behavior*, *18*, 176-180.

Lester, D. (1988b). Restricting the availability of guns as a strategy for suicide prevention. *Biology & Society*, *5*, 127-129.

Lester, D. (1992). *Why people kill themselves (3rd ed.).* Springfield, IL: Charles C. Thomas.

Lester, D. (1995). Preventing suicide in women and men. *Crisis*, *16*, 79-84.

Lester, D. (1996). Gun ownership and rates of homicide and suicide. *European Journal of Psychiatry*, *10*, 83-85.

Lester, D. (2000a). *Why people kill themselves: A 2000 summary of research on suicide*. Springfield, IL: Charles C. Thomas.

Lester, D. (2000b). Gun availibity and the use of guns for suicide and homicide in Canada. *Canadian Journal of Public Health*, *91*, 186-187.

Lester, D. & Leenaars, A. (1993). Suicide rates in Canada before and after tightening firearm control laws. *Psychological Reports*, *72*, 787-790.

Lester, D. & Leenaars, A. (1994). Gun control and rates of firearm violence in Canada and the United States. *Canadian Journal of Criminology*, *36*, 463-464.

Lipset, S. (1990). *Continental divide.* New York, NY: Routledge.

Ludwig, J. & Cook, P. (2000). Homicide and suicide rates associated with implementation of the Brady Handgun Violence Protection Act. *Journal of the American Medical Association (JAMA)*, *284*, 585-591.

Malcolm, A. (1988, November, 20). Canada's deeper identity not made in the U.S.A. *New York Times*, pp. 1, 18.

Mann, J., Apter, A., Bertolotte, J, Beautrias, A., Currier, D., Hass, A., Hegerl, U., et al. (2005). Suicide prevention strategies: A systematic review. *The Journal of The American Medical Association (JAMA)*, *294*, 2064-2074.

Markush, R. & Bertolucci, A. (1984). Firearms and suicide in the United States. *American Journal of Public Health*, *74*, 123-127.

Maxwell, S., Stolensky, D., Goodman, N., Sommers, P. & Boyd, J. (1984). Suicide by firearms. *New England Journal of Medicine*, *310*, 46-49.

Medoff, M. & Magaddino, J. (1983). Suicides and firearm control laws. *Evaluation Review*, *7*, 357-372.

Meehl, P. (1986). Diagnostic taxa as open concepts. Metatheoretical and statistical questions about reliability and construct validity in the grand strategy of nosological revision. In T. Millon & G. Klerman (Eds.) (2010), *Contemporary directions in psychopathology*, (pp. 215–231). New York, NY: Guilford. (Reprinted).

Millon, T. (2010). Classification considerations in psychopathology and personality. In T. Millon, R. Kruger, & E. Simonson (Eds.), *Contemporary directions in psychopathology*, (pp. 149-173). New York, NY: Guilford.

Miller, M. & Hemenway, D. (1999). The relationship between firearms and suicide: A review of the literature. *Aggression and Violent Behavior*, *4*, 59-75.

Mundt, D. (1990). Gun control and rates of firearm violence in Canada and the United States. *Canadian Journal of Criminology*, *32*, 137-154.

Platt, S. (1984). Unemployment and suicidal behavior. *Social Science & Medicine*, *19*, 93-115.

Rich, C., Young, J., Fowler, R., Wagner, J. & Black, N. (1990). Guns and suicide. *American Journal of Psychiatry*, *147*, 342-346.

Richman, J. (1993). *Preventing elderly suicide*. New York: Springer.

Royal Canadian Mounted Police. (2010). *RCMP Canadian Firearms Program. Program Evaluation.* Ottawa: Author.

Shneidman, E. (1973a). *Deaths of man*. New York, NY: Quadrangle.

Shneidman, E. (1973b). Suicide. In *Encyclopedia Britannica*, *21*, 383–385. Chicago, IL: Williams Benton.

Shneidman, E. (1985). *Definition of suicide*. New York, NY: John Wiley & Sons.

Shneidman, E. & Farberow, N. (Eds.). (1957). *Clues to suicide*. New York: McGraw-Hill.

Sloan, J., Rivera, F., Reay, D., Feris, J. & Kellerman, A. (1990). Firearm regulation and rates of suicide: A comparison of two metropolitan areas. *New England Journal of Medicine*, *322*, 369-373.

Sommers, P. (1984). The effect of gun control laws on suicide rates. *Atlantic Economic Journal*, *12*, 67-69.

Stack, S. (1998). Research on controlling suicide: Methodological issues. *Archives of Suicide Research*, *4*, 95-99.

Stengel, E. (1964). *Suicide and attempted suicide.* Baltimore: Penguin.

Tugwell, P. & Knottnerus, J. (2015). Is the 'Evidence-Pyramid' now dead? *Journal of Clinical Epidemiology*, *68*, 1247-1250.

Weber, M. (1949). *The methodology of social sciences.* (E. Shils & H. Fich, Trans. And Eds.) Glencoe, ILL: The Free Press. (Original essays written between 1903 to 1917).

World Health Organization (WHO). (2002). *World report on violence and health*. Geneva, Switzerland: Author.

World Health Organization (WHO). (2006). *Preventing disease through healthy environments.* Geneva, Switzerland: Author.

World Health Organization (WHO). (2014). *Suicide prevention: A global imperative*. Geneva, Switzerland: Author.

Zachar, P. & Kendler, K. (2010). Philosophical issues in the classification of psychopathology. In T. Millon, R. Krueger, & E. Simonson (Eds.), *Contemporary directions in psychopathology*, (pp. 127-148). New York, NY: Guilford Press.

In: Firearms and Suicide
Editor: David Lester
ISBN: 978-1-53614-690-5


*Chapter 5*

# GUN CONTROL IN AUSTRALIA

***Karolina Krysinska, PhD[1,*] and David Lester, PhD[2]***
[1]University of Melbourne, Melbourne, Australia
[2]Stockton University, Galloway, NJ, US

## ABSTRACT

Australia passed a strict gun control law in 1996 (National Firearms Agreement) in response to a mass murder incident. Although there are dissenting studies, the majority of the research shows a reduction in the firearm suicide rate, without any indication that potential suicides switched to alternative methods. Age, gender, geographical location, occupation, and psychosocial factors, including mental health, appear to play a role in choosing firearms as means of ending one's own life.

Occasional research on the impact of access to firearms has been conducted in nations, such as Australia, which is of interest because attitudes toward guns and gun control differ by nation. For example, in a survey of college students, Cooke (2004) found that students in Australia and the United Kingdom scored lower than American students on questions

---

* Corresponding Author Email: karolina.krysinska@unimelb.edu.au.

measuring whether they favored gun possession, on whether people have a right to own a gun, and on whether possession of a gun provides protection from crime. They scored higher on the belief that guns stimulate crime.

The role of gun control and gun availability in Australia is of particular interest because the country moved from having individual state and territory laws prior to 1996 to a nationwide gun control law thereafter. This chapter starts with an overview of suicide methods in Australia over the last thirty years. It is followed by presenting the National Firearms Agreement (NFA) introduced in 1996 and results of studies investigating whether the NFA had an impact on firearm suicide in Australia. The next section reviews Australian studies shedding light on the choice of suicide methods, and the chapter ends with conclusions regarding the impact of gun control in Australia on firearm suicide in the country, including method substitution.

## SUICIDE METHODS IN AUSTRALIA

In 2016, 2,866 people died from suicide in Australia, which results in a suicide rate of 11.7 per 100,000 persons per year (Australian Bureau of Statistics, 2017). The suicide rate in males was higher than the suicide rate in females by 3:1 (17.8 vs. 5.8). In 2016, suicide was the leading cause of death in younger age groups (15-44 years of age) and the second leading cause of death among people aged 45-54 years. Between 1986 and 2005, firearms accounted for 16% of total suicides in Australia (Qi, et al., 2014). Other major suicide methods were hanging (35%), gases and vapors (20%), and solid or liquid substances (15%). There were differences between gender and age groups in the methods of suicide used over this period, as well as differences in methods used in different geographical areas of Australia. Males died mostly by self-inflicted hanging, firearms, gases and self-poisoning. Females used hanging and self-poisoning most frequently. Although firearm suicide rates, and rates of suicide by solid and liquid substances, decreased over 1986-2005, especially among people aged 15–54 years and in rural and remote areas, suicide by hanging increased, especially among people aged 15–54 years. In older age groups (55+ years), suicide rates by hanging and firearms remained relatively stable. In addition, firearm suicide rates were higher in rural areas than in urban locations, and the trend was reversed for suicide by self-poisoning (Qi, et al., 2014).

The significant drop in firearm suicide in Australia over the last three decades was also reported by Ajdacic Gross, et al. (2006) who used World Health Organization data for their analysis of firearm suicide around the world. Although the crude total suicide rates in Australia remained relatively stable between 1983 and 2000 (11.6 and 12.8, respectively), in 1983 firearm suicides accounted for 29.5% of all suicides in Australia, and this proportion dropped to 18.6% in 1993 and 10.2% in 2000.

More recently, Spittal, et al. (2012) investigated the relationship between the number of suicide deaths and changes in suicide methods and their lethality in Australia over the period 1994-2007. Their analysis included the three most lethal suicide methods in the country: hanging (42% of total suicides), motor vehicle exhaust (19%) and firearms (11%). They found that firearms were the most lethal suicide method: 74.2% of suicide acts using this method led to death, while hanging was the second most lethal method (59.1%). Spittal, et al. attributed the decrease in firearm suicides over the period to a lower rate of suicide acts using firearms, which decreased from 0.6 per 100,000 in 1994 to 0.4 per 100,000 in 2007 (RR= 0.96 per year, 95% CI 0.93–0.98). There was a small change in the lethality of these attempts (RR = 0.99 per year, 95% CI 0.98–1.00).

## STUDIES IN AUSTRALIA PRIOR TO 1996

Lester (1988) studied six Australian states in 1975-1977 and correlated the number of guns per capita and the percentage of households owning guns with the suicide rate and the homicide rate. For males, the more guns in the state, the higher the firearm suicide rate, the lower the suicide rate by all other methods and the higher the percentages of suicides using guns. For homicide, the more guns in the state, the higher the percentage of homicides using guns. The percentage of households owning guns was more strongly associated with the suicide and homicide measures than was the number of guns per capita. Lester showed that the results for the six Australian states paralleled the results for the nine major regions of the United States for the same period.

Snowdon and Harris (1992) conducted a similar study. They studied suicide in five Australian states for the period 1968 to 1989. (They could not obtain reliable data for the Northern Territories or the Australian Capital Territory, and they omitted Tasmania.) The use of firearms for suicide was primarily a male choice, with male firearm suicide rates in 1989 ranging from 3.8 per 100,000 per year in Western Australia to 8.4 in Queensland. In contrast, the female firearm suicide rate in 1989 ranged from 0.1 in Western Australia to 0.6 in South Australia. Snowdon and Harris had estimates for the percentage of households with guns in 1975 and average annual male firearm suicide rates for 1968 to 1989. The Spearman rank correlation coefficient (calculated by David Lester) between the two variables is 0.9, which is statistically significant at the one-tailed 5% level.

Cantor and Lewin (1990) reported a more extensive analysis of the use of guns for suicide in Australia for the period 1961-1985. During this period, the total suicide rate declined, but the firearm suicide rate remained stable, with the result that the proportion of suicides using firearms increased. Young males showed an increasing use of guns for suicide. In their regional analysis, Cantor and Lewin added Tasmania and used measures of guns per 1,000 persons and the percentage of households owning a gun. Both measures were positively (but non-significantly) associated with the proportion of suicides using guns in the six states for males and for females.

During this period, South Australia passed a gun control law in 1977 which was implemented in 1980. This law required gun owners to be licensed and pass an exam on the safety and handling of weapons. The firearm suicide rate in South Australia declined from 1968-1979 to 1980-1989 (from 6.7 to 5.8), whereas it rose in the four other states (from 5.4 to 6.1). However, the suicide rate by all other methods rose in South Australia (from 9.6 to 12.8), as it did in the four other states (from 11.0 to 12.6). The total suicide rate, therefore, rose from 16.3 to 18.6 in South Australia and from 16.4 to 18.7 in the four other states. The question of whether, when gun ownership was restricted, people switched to other methods for suicide cannot easily be answered by these data.

Cantor and Slater (1995) studied Queensland in the two years prior and after passage of a weapons act that required the purchase of a license to buy a long gun, a waiting period, and a examination on safety. Pre-existing long gun owners also had to acquire a license. The number of suicides using guns declined significantly for men (very few women used guns for suicide), in those of all ages and in metropolitan areas and provincial cities but not in rural areas. The total number of suicides by men declined also, mainly in the provincial cities.

## THE 1996 GUN LAW

On April 28, 1996, Martin Bryant, a lone gunman with a semi-automatic weapon, killed 35 people and seriously injured 18 people in Port Arthur, Tasmania. In response, in 1996, the Commonwealth, states and territories in Australia implemented the National Firearms Agreement (NFA), followed in 2002 by the National Handgun Control Agreement (Leigh & Neill, 2010). The NFA banned semi-automatic rifles and semi-automatic and pump action shotguns and introduced strict requirements for the possession of firearms. These included the necessity of having a proven reason (i.e., "genuine reason") to own a firearm (with explicit exclusion of self-defense), 28-day waiting periods for acquisitions of firearms, and compulsory written safety tests. The NFA stipulated safe storage and registration of privately-owned firearms through a state-controlled firearms management agency. The reforms also included compulsory government buy-backs of the banned weapons with financial compensation at market prices. Between 1991 and 2006 the Australian gun buy-back was the largest destruction of civilian firearms worldwide and resulted in the collection of over 650,000 firearms at an estimated cost of AU$500 (Commonwealth of Australia, 1997).

## The Impact of the 1996 Gun Law

Reuter and Mouzos (2003) attempted to analyze the impact of the buy-back program and passage of the NFA but, not only did they not employ any statistical techniques (they merely charted the trends in suicide and homicide during the period involved), but it is impossible to evaluate the effects of the buy-back program separately from the passage of the gun control laws. Reviewing a number of unpublished studies from the Australian Institute of Criminology, they noted that: (1) firearm-related homicides declined even more sharply after the NFA while the proportion of homicides using guns increased, (2) firearm suicide rates declined before and after the NFA with no noticeable change in the decline after the NRA, (3) accidental firearm injuries including hospitalization for such injuries, declined after the NFA, (4) attempted murder using firearms remained stable and showed little change, (5) armed robberies increased during the period, but the use of guns in those robberies declined after the NFA, and (6) the number of firearms stolen declined after the NFA.

Chapman, Alpers, Agho and Jones (2006) studied the impact of the 1996 national gun control law. They found that:

1) The rate of total firearm deaths was declining by 3% per year prior to 1996 and by 6% after 1996.
2) The rate of firearm suicides was declining by 3% per year prior to 1996 and by 7.4% after 1996.
3) The rate of firearm homicides was declining by 3% per year prior to 1996 and by 7.5% after 1996.
4) The rate of accidental firearms deaths was declining by 7.6% per year prior to 1996 but *increased* by 8.5% after 1996.

More recently Chapman, Alpers and Jones (2016) conducted a follow-up study using data covering a longer period of time (1979-2013). They reported that the rate of total deaths due to firearms declined from 3.6 per

100,000 pre-1996 to 1.2 post-1996. The mean annual firearm suicide rate declined from 3 pre-1996 to 0.99 post-1996, while the rates of non-firearm suicide and total suicides remained relatively stable over both time periods (9.2 vs 10.7 and 12.2 vs 11.7; respectively). The rate of firearm suicide was declining by 3% per year prior to 1996 and by 4.8% per year after 1996. In other words, although firearm suicide declined even before the NFA, this drop increased significantly after 1996, and no method substitution was detected either for suicide or homicide.

Thus, the 1996 law reduced firearm deaths for both suicide and homicide, but not for accidental deaths. This latter phenomenon was based on very small numbers of deaths, and McPhedran and Baker (2008) suggested that it was a result of coroners classifying more suicides as unintentional deaths and, even if the verdict was eventually corrected, the Australian Bureau of Statistics failing to tabulate accurate statistics on deaths (De Leo, 2007).

What of switching to other methods for homicide and suicide (McPhedran & Baker, 2008)? The total non-firearm homicide rate was increasing by 1.1% per year prior to 1996 but declined by 2.4% after 1996. The total homicide rate was stable prior to 1996 and declined after 1996. Thus, no switching of method occurred for homicide.

The non-firearm suicide rate was increasing at 2.3% per year prior to 1996 and declined by 4.1% after 1996. The total suicide rate was stable prior to 1996 and declined after 1996. No evidence was found, therefore, that switching of methods occurred for suicide.

Baker and McPhedran (2007) used a different statistical technique (the ARIMA or Box-Jenkins model) and found that firearm suicide rates declined significantly more than predicted after the passage of the NFA. The suicide rate by all other methods did not differ from predictions, except for 1997 and 1998 when this rate was higher than expected, but not thereafter. Homicide rates by firearms and by all other methods did not differ from predictions, and so the NFA did not appear to have an impact on homicides. Finally, their analysis showed that the observed rate of accidental firearm death was higher than predicted.

In line with earlier studies (Baker & McPhedran, 2007; Chapman, et al, 2006), Baker and McPhedran (2015) carried out an ARIMA analysis on a longer time series of mortality data to predict annual firearm suicide and firearm homicide for the years 1997 to 2010. They found a decline in firearm suicide rates both pre- and post-NFA. However, the observed suicide rates between 1997 and 2010 were consistently (and significantly) lower than the predicted values. There was also a substantial and significant decline in non-firearm suicide post-NFA. Baker and McPhedran reported no significant differences between the observed and predicted firearm homicide trends. The study did not include an analysis of data regarding possible method substitution.

Neill and Leigh (2007) revisited the data analysis by Baker and McPhedran (2007). They tested whether the findings of Baker and McPhedran could be replicated using (i) a longer time series, and (ii) the log of the death rate instead of the actual rate. They found that reanalyzing data using a longer time series (1915-2004 vs 1979-1996) provided stronger evidence for the effect of NFA on both firearm and firearm homicide. In case of firearm suicide, there were 247 Lives Saved per Year for the former and 126 for the later time series (for firearm homicide: 36 vs 7; respectively). Neill and Leigh also showed an increase in the predicted death rate in the log model compared with the levels models used by Baker and McPhedran. Consequently, in the case of firearm suicide, they found 233 Lives Saved per Year versus 26 (for firearm homicide: 35 vs 2; respectively). In regard to the possibility of changing the suicide method in absence of available firearms, Neill and Leigh concluded that the "fact that overall violent deaths have fallen since 1996 - even accounting for the Port Arthur effect - suggests there has not been substantial method substitution" (p. 10).

Lee and Suardi (2010) observed that although studies presented above (Baker & McPhedran, 2007; Chapman, et al., 2006; Neill & Leigh, 2007; Reuter & Mouzos, 2003) used the same data sources from the Australian Bureau of Statistics (ABS), there has been no consensus regarding the NFA impact on firearm suicide and firearm homicide rates in the country. They reanalyzed these mortality data for 1915–2004 applying a battery of tests for unknown structural breaks, and they found no evidence suggesting that the NFA had any significant effects on firearm suicide, non-firearm suicide, firearm homicide or non-firearm homicide. Neither did they find any method substitution effect. It appears that conclusions about the impact of the 1996 law depend upon the statistical techniques used for the analysis.

McPhedran and Baker (2012) confirmed the finding of a lack of structural breaks in firearm suicide around the time of NFA reported by Lee and Suardi (2010). They looked at mortality data for firearm, hanging, and other suicide methods over the periods 1907-2007 and 1979–2007 for three age groups: 15 to 24, 25 to 34, and 35 to 44 years of age. Using a battery of statistical tests, McPhedran and Baker found structural breaks in firearm suicide prior to the NFA introduced in 1996, which seems to support an observation of long-term decreasing trends in firearm suicide in Australia. Across the age groups, there was no evidence of a change possibly related to the NFA among the two younger age groups (15 to 24 and 25 to 34 year-olds). There was some evidence of a structural break in firearm suicides shortly after 1996 for the 35 to 44 year-old group. However, around the same time a similar break was found in suicides by hanging. The study did not look at the phenomenon of method substitution.

Instead of analyzing time-series variations, Leigh and Neill (2010) used an alternative approach for studying the effect of the Australian firearms buy-back program. They looked at the variation over time and across Australian states and territories to answer the question of whether firearm death rates decreased more substantially in areas where more guns were withdrawn in the NFA buy-back program. Plotting the change in the number of guns (per 100,000 population) against the change in firearm suicide and firearm homicide rates for the periods 1990-1995 and 1998-2003 showed a negative relationship between the buy-back rate and firearm-related mortality. The authors estimated that buying back 3,500 guns per 100,000 population reduced the firearm suicide death rate by 1.9 per 100,000. This represented a 74% decline and 376 fewer firearm suicides per year in Australia (with a population of around 20 million at the time the study was conducted). There was also a negative relationship between the firearm homicide death rate (34% decline and 31 fewer deaths). This effect was not found for non-firearm suicide or homicide deaths. The method used by Leigh and Neill does not allow us to conclude whether there was any method substitution effect.

Klieve, Barnes and De Leo (2008) looked at the impact of the 1996 NFA on male suicide in Australia and in Queensland where a suicide register has been established to monitor suicides more accurately. The results for Queensland and Australia are similar, namely, a steady declining firearm suicide rate from 1990 to 2004, combined with a steadily increasing suicide rate by hanging. Klieve, et al. observed that the downward trends in the firearm suicide rate in Queensland in 1990-1996 and 1997-2004 were not significantly different. However, visual inspection of their graphs shows a noticeable discontinuity in the period 1996-1998. Klieve, et al. noted that the age of those using hanging declined over the period while the age of those using firearms increased. This suggests that younger males turned to hanging more while older males continued to use firearms.

Ozanne-Smith, et al. (2004) reported changes in firearm-related deaths in Victoria as compared to the rest of Australia. Victoria tightened restrictions on semi-automatic guns in 1988, whereas the rest of Australia did not do so. In 1996, along with the other Australian states, Victoria adopted the national firearm standards. From 1988 to 1995, Victoria experienced a 17.3% reduction in firearm deaths relative to Australia, and this was significant for all firearm deaths and for firearm suicides, but not for firearm homicide and unintentional firearm deaths. After 1997, Australia experienced a 14% reduction in firearm deaths relative to Victoria, so that Australia as a whole "caught up" with the decline in Victoria.

Incidentally, Ozanne-Smith, et al. noted that, in 1998 as compared to 1992, household ownership of guns and ammunition declined in Melbourne, and the number of registered firearms and owners in Victoria also declined. (The buyback program in Australia lasted from September 1996 to September 1997).

## Studies Relevant to Switching Methods for Suicide

De Leo, Evans and Neulinger (2002) compared men using hanging, firearms and non-domestic gas (mainly car exhaust) for suicide in Queensland in 1994-1996. They found differences in the personal and social characteristics of the suicides. Those using non-domestic gas more often lived alone and left a suicide note, those using firearms had less often made previous attempts at suicide, while those using hanging were more often psychotic and younger. Thus, different types of people choose the various methods for suicide, and this suggests (but does not prove) that changing the availability of a method for suicide would affect only some sub-groups of the population.

One problem in examining the availability of one single method of suicide over time is that the availability of other methods changes too. If guns are made less readily available, there may be changes in car ownership and type of car owned, changes in emission controls on cars, changes in the availability and toxicity of domestic gas, fencing in bridges and other high buildings, and restrictions on medications (both prescribed and over-the-counter) and pesticides at the same time. No study has examined changes in the availability of several methods of suicide during the same period of time.

However, changes in method for suicide have been documented over time. De Leo, Dwyer, Firman and Neulinger (2003) noted that, from 1975 to 1998 in Australia for men, the suicide rate by firearm declined while the suicide rate by hanging increased. The data presented by these authors also showed an increase in the use of "other gases" (that is, car exhaust). The overall male suicide rate increased during this time period. The largest change was the increase in the use of hanging for suicide and, obviously, access to this method for suicide cannot be restricted. De Leo, et al. argued that their data showed that substitution of method had occurred in Australia as the availability of guns was restricted.

In a population study exploring firearm accessibility and method choice, Klieve, Sveticic and De Leo (2009) looked at factors impacting the choice of firearms as a means of suicide. Based on Queensland suicide data for

1997-2004, they observed that the firearm suicide rate in individuals with a gun license history greatly exceeded the firearm suicide rate in people with no license history (10.9 per 100,000 vs 1.03 per 100,000). Older males from rural locations comprised a group with the highest risk of selecting firearms as means of suicide. In addition, a history of current of present firearms license doubled the risk of suicide by any means.

Milner, et al. (2017) conducted a retrospective study (2001-2012) to explore whether suicide rates for males and females in Australia differed between occupations with access to lethal means (firearms, medicines/drugs and carbon monoxide) and occupations without such access. They found that individuals in occupations with access to lethal means frequently used these methods in suicide, and this effect was particularly strong in females (IRR=3.02 vs. IRR=1.24 for males). In case of occupations with access to firearms, such as farmers, defense force workers, fire and emergency staff, prison officers, police, security officers and guards, 30.4% of males and 17.4% of females used this means to end their lives. Access to and familiarity with firearms have also been reported as a significant environmental risk factor for suicide in Australian farmers in a recent qualitative study (Perceval, et al., 2018). In the words of one of the study participants, "that may be why suicide is at a higher rate in the country, because we do that (use firearms) on a daily basis anyway. It's an identified end to a problem for everything else" (p. 4).

## CONCLUSION

There is evidence that introduction of strict gun control laws in Australia in 1996 had a significant impact on the incidence of firearm suicide in the country. A number of studies presented in this chapter showed that limiting access to this highly lethal suicide method has reduced firearm suicide rates and that no method substitution has been reported. Age, gender, geographical location, occupation, and psychosocial factors, including mental health, play a role in choosing firearms as means of ending one's own life. Access to, familiarity with and (perceived) lethality of firearms also play a significant role in this process, similar to the process of selecting other suicide methods. Despite these general positive findings, some studies (Lee & Suardi, 2010) either did not report changes in firearm suicide rates around the time that the NFA was introduced or found a decline in selected subpopulations (McPhedran & Baker, 2012). These divergent findings reported in Australia may be artefacts of statistical methods or data sets used, as well as a reflection of the complexity of means restriction effects.

## REFERENCES

Australian Bureau of Statistics (2017). *3302.0 - Deaths, Australia, 2016.* Canberra: ABS.

Ajdacic-Gross, V., Killias, M., Hepp, U., Gadola, E., Bopp, M., Lauber, C., ... & Rössler, W. (2006). Changing times: a longitudinal analysis of international firearm suicide data. *American Journal of Public Health, 96*, 1752-1755.

Baker, J., & McPhedran, S. (2007). Gun laws and sudden death. *British Journal of Criminology*, 47, 455-469.

Baker, J., & McPhedran, S. (2015). Australian firearm related deaths: new findings and implications for crime prevention and health policies following revisions to official death count data. *International Journal of Criminal Justice Sciences, 10*(1), 1-9.

Cantor, C. H., & Slater, P. J. (1995). The impact of firearm control legislation on suicide in Queensland. *Medical Journal of Australia*, 162, 583-585.

Cantor, C. H., & Lewin, T. (1990). Firearms and suicide in Australia. *Australian & New Zealand Journal of Psychiatry*, 24, 500-509.

Chapman, S., Alpers, P., Agho, K., & Jones, M. (2006). Australia's 1996 gun law reforms. *Injury Prevention*, 12, 365-372.

Chapman, S., Alpers, P., & Jones, M. (2016). Association between gun law reforms and intentional firearm deaths in Australia, 1979-2013. *Journal of the American Medical Association, 316*, 291-299.

Commonwealth of Australia (1997). *The gun buy-back scheme*. Canberra: Australian National Audit Office. Accessed 21 August 2018 from: https://www.anao.gov.au/work/performance-audit/gun-buy-back-scheme.

Cooke, C. A. (2004). Young people's attitudes towards guns in America, Great Britain, and Western Australia. *Aggressive Behavior*, 30, 93-104.

De Leo, D. (2007). Suicide mortality data needs revision. *Medical Journal of Australia*, 186, 157.

De Leo, D., Dwyer, J., Firman, D., & Neulinger, K. (2003). Trends in hanging and firearm suicide rates in Australia. *Suicide & Life-Threatening Behavior*, 33, 151-164.

De Leo, D., Evans, R., & Neulinger, K. (2002). Hanging, firearm, and non-domestic gas suicides among males. *Australian & New Zealand Journal of Psychiatry*, 36, 183-189.

Klieve, H., Barnes, M., & De Leo, D. (2008). Controlling firearms use in Australia. *Social Psychiatry & Psychiatric Epidemiology*, 44, 285-292.

Klieve, H., Sveticic, J., & De Leo, D. (2009). Who uses firearms as a means of suicide? A population study exploring firearm accessibility and method choice. *BMC Medicine, 7*(1), 52.

Lee, W-S, & Suardi, S. (2010). The Australian firearms buyback and its effect on gun deaths. *Contemporary Economic Policy, 28*, 65-79.

Leigh, A., & Neill, C. (2010). Do gun buybacks save lives? Evidence from panel data. *American Law and Economics Review, 12*, 509-557.

Lester, D. (1988). Restricting the availability of guns as a strategy for preventing suicide. *Biology & Society*, 5, 127-129.

McPhedran, S., & Baker, J. (2008). Australian firearms legislation and unintentional firearm deaths. *Journal of Public Health*, 122, 297-299.

McPhedran, S., & Baker, J. (2012). Suicide prevention and method restriction: Evaluating the impact of limiting access to lethal means among young Australians. *Archives of Suicide Research, 16*, 135-146.

Milner, A., Witt, K., Maheen, H., & LaMontagne, A. D. (2017). Access to means of suicide, occupation and the risk of suicide: A national study over 12 years of coronial data. *BMC Psychiatry, 17*, 125.

Neill, C., & Leigh, A. (2007). *Weak tests and strong conclusions: A re-analysis of gun deaths and the Australian firearms buyback. Discussion Paper 555*. Canberra: Australian National University. Accessed 21 August 2018 from: https://openresearch-repository.anu.edu.au/bitstream/1885/45285/3/DP555.pdf.

Ozanne-Smith, J., Ashby, K., Newstead, S., Stathakis, V. Z., & Clapperton, A. (2004). Firearm related deaths. *Injury Prevention*, 10, 280-286.

Perceval, M., Kõlves, K., Ross, V., Reddy, P., & De Leo, D. (2018). Environmental factors and suicide in Australian farmers: A qualitative study. *Archives of Environmental & Occupational Health*, in press.

Qi, X., Hu, W., Page, A., & Tong, S. (2014). Dynamic pattern of suicide in Australia, 1986–2005: A descriptive-analytic study. *BMJ Open, 4*(7), e005311.

Reuter, P., & Mouzos, J. (2003). Australia. In J. Ludwig & P. J. Cook (Eds.) *Evaluating gun policy*, pp. 121-156. Washington, DC: Brookings Institute Press.

Spittal, M. J., Pirkis, J., Miller, M., & Studdert, D. M. (2012). Declines in the lethality of suicide attempts explain the decline in suicide deaths in Australia. *PLoS One, 7*(9), e44565.

Snowdon, J., & Harris, L. (1992). Firearms suicides in Australia. *Medical Journal of Australia*, 156, 79-88.

In: Firearms and Suicide
Editor: David Lester
ISBN: 978-1-53614-690-5


*Chapter 6*

# CONCLUSION

***David Lester****
Stockton University, Galloway, New Jersey, US

## ABSTRACT

This chapter presents conclusions from the earlier chapters. Frameworks for evaluating efforts to prevent suicide are presented and suggestions made for realistic proposals for preventing suicide by firearms.

## WILLIAM HADDON'S COUNTER MEASURES FOR REDUCING HAZARDS

Runyan, Brown and Brooks-Russell (2015) applied William Haddon's (1973) countermeasures for reducing hazards to firearm suicides.

- *Countermeasure 1*: Prevent the creation of the hazard. For firearm suicide, this would entail not producing firearms.

* Corresponding Author Email: lesterd@stockton.edu.

- *Countermeasure 2*: Reduce the amount of hazard brought into being. For firearm suicide this would mean reducing the number of firearms allowed to be sold or purchased.
- *Countermeasure 3*: Prevent the release of the hazard. For firearm suicide, this might entail installing locks on firearms.
- *Countermeasure 4*: Modify the rate of release of the hazard from its sources. For firearm suicide, this would entail eliminating automatic firearms. However, it has been noted in an earlier chapter that the use of automatic firearms for suicide is relatively uncommon.
- *Countermeasure 5*: Separate the hazard from that which is to be protected by time and space. For firearm suicide, this might be achieved by storing firearms at gun clubs rather than at home.
- *Countermeasure 6*: Separate the hazard from that which is to be protected by a physical barrier. For preventing firearm suicides, this could include keeping firearms unloaded and in locked containers with ammunition stored separately.
- *Countermeasure 7*: Modify relevant basic qualities of the hazard. For firearm suicide, this might entail personalizing firearms so that they can be fired only by the owner.
- *Countermeasure 8*: Make what is to be protected more resistant to damage from the hazard. Creating and marketing bullet-proof garments would fit with this countermeasure, but this is relevant to preventing the shooting of others rather than oneself.
- *Countermeasure 9*: Begin to counter damage by the hazard. Provide good access to emergency care in the pre-hospital period.
- *Countermeasure 10*: Stabilize, repair and rehabilitate the object of damage. Provide high quality trauma care in hospitals.

These examples of countermeasures are that, only examples. Other tactics for preventing firearm suicides might be possible for each countermeasure. However, they provide a useful framework for thinking about preventing firearm suicide. In particular, countermeasures 3, 5, 6 and 7 appear to be the most viable for preventing firearm suicide. Making firearms safer for example, by installing locks on guns, separating the firearms from potential abusers (such as storing firearms at gun clubs), safe storage at home, and personalizing firearms by designing them so that only the owner can fire them all seem to be useful for preventing firearm suicide, although storing firearms at gun clubs is unlikely to be approved by firearm owners in the United States.

## PREVENTING FIREARM SUICIDE IN THE MILITARY

We have seen in earlier chapter that two programs to prevent soldiers from easy access to firearms for suicide have been successful. In Israel, soldiers were no longer allowed to take their firearms home on leave. They were required to leave their firearms on the base. The number of suicides dropped from 28 per year prior to this change to 16.5 after the change (Lubin, et al., 2010). Switzerland, reduced the age at which military service ended from 43 to 33 and recruited fewer soldiers. The result was that fewer Swiss residents stored firearms at home. The firearm suicide rate in Switzerland dropped by 27% after this change (Reisch, et al., 2013).

Hoyt and Duffy (2015) discussed what measures might be taken in the United States that would help prevent firearm suicides among the military. They note that, despite Second Amendment rights, firearms can be restricted to certain classes of people, such as the mentally ill, given specific processes such as court rulings. The military has also instituted rules, such as restricting soldiers from carrying a firearm if there is a history of domestic violence, and limitations have been imposed for drug addiction and dishonorable discharges. Hoyt and Duffy made five recommendations for commanders.

1. Provide space in arms room for voluntary, short-term storage of privately owned firearms
2. Require registration with the Provost Marshall of all privately-owned firearms stored on the base
3. Emphasize weapons safety such as safe storage

4. If soldiers are restricted from firearm use, reduce the stigma involved by providing gainful employment on the base.
5. As a last resort, restrict a soldier to the base in order to temporarily prevent access to privately-owned firearms stored off-base. This requires the soldier to obey the restriction, which may not happen.

As in other proposals in this chapter, the appropriateness of the tactic or recommendation depends on whether the individual voluntarily complies. Recommendation 1 above has to be voluntary, while recommendation 2 can be required. A recommendation that privately-owned firearms be stored at gun clubs with secure lockers can only be voluntary. Hoyt and Duffy also note that, to be effective, the choices made by commanders depend on having mental health staff (on-base or off-base) who are competent at assessing suicidal risk and on having good communication channels between the mental health staff and commanders.

## The 2018 Rand Corporation Report

The Rand Corporation (2018) produced a report that reviewed the impact of gun policies on suicide, violent crime, unintentional deaths, mass shootings, and the gun industry. The following sections will review the conclusions for firearm suicide, but it must be noted that the author of the reviews on this issue (Rajeev Ramchand) found very few studies that met the criteria for sound research.

### Background Checks

Studies on the impact of background checks (for domestic violence, mental illness, fugitive status and misdemeanors) produced moderate evidence for an impact on firearm suicides and limited evidence for the impact on the total number of suicides. However, the research on background checks was limited by the fact that other firearm policies were typically instituted at the same time.

## Restrictions of the Sale of Assault Weapons

There were no impacts noted of this policy on firearm suicides, consistent with my comments in the Preface to the present book that automatic firearms are rarely used for suicide.

## Stand your Ground Laws

Although this policy would be expected to have no impact on firearm suicides, The Rand report found one study that had some data, but the result was inconclusive.

## Mental Illness Prohibitions

The results of the limited research on this policy provided only limited evidence for its impact on firearm suicides and the total number of suicides

## Requirements for Reporting Lost or Stolen Firearms

There was no research on the impact of this policy on firearm suicide.

## Licensing and Permitting Requirements

The evidence for an impact of these requirements was inconclusive

## Firearm Sales Reporting and Recording Requirements

There was no research on the impact of this policy on firearm suicide.

## Child Access Prevention Laws

The research reviewed provided moderate evidence for a preventive impact on firearm suicides and, in addition, supportive evidence for a preventive impact on suicide attempts.

## Surrender of Firearms by Prohibited Possessor

There was no research on the impact of this policy on firearm suicide.

## Minimum Age Requirements

The research on the impact of this policy was inconclusive for firearm suicides in general and the total number of suicides, but the research provided limited evidence that the policy had an impact on firearm suicide in children and adolescents.

## Concealed Carry Laws

The research on the impact of this policy was inconclusive for firearm suicides and the total number of suicides.

## Waiting Periods

There was no research on the impact of this policy on firearm suicide.

### Gun-Free Zones

There was no research on the impact of this policy on firearm suicide.

In my books on the deterrent effect of capital punishment on murder rates, I suggested that it was important for reviewers to state their position on capital punishment since the reviewer's views might affect their reading of and interpretation of the research. In Chapter 3 of the present book, John Gunn stated his position as gun owner and his involvement with suicide prevention. I do not know the personal position of the reviewer(s) in the Rand Corporation report. In favor of the conclusions of the review, the reviewer did examine the methodology of each study and mentioned the limitations of each study. To sum up the conclusions of the review, the author concluded that there was moderate evidence for the effectiveness of child access prevention laws, and limited evidence for the impact of mental illness prohibitions and minimum age requirements. Both of these policies should be acceptable to gun-related organizations.

The Rand Corporation Report also reviewed research on other aspects of firearms and suicide. The research available indicated that firearm availability does impact firearm suicides and the total number of suicides. However, there were limitations in the methodology of the research. As will be mentioned below, there are restrictions placed on government funding for research on the use of firearms for suicide, homicide and accidental deaths by the American government. This impedes research into these issues. To have such restrictions in a modern country is reprehensible and inexcusable, and these restrictions should be removed.

## Collaboration between Gun Rights and Suicide Prevention Organizations

John Gunn argued in Chapter 3 that collaboration between gun rights and suicide prevention organizations is possible and should be pursued. Morral, et al. (2018) provided some support for such collaborations. In their study of the opinions of experts both sides of the gun policy debate, they found that there were some policies for which the two groups were in relative agreement, including expanded mental health prohibitions (against gun ownership), required reporting of lost and stolen firearms, media campaigns to prevent child access, and surrender of firearms by prohibited possessors. There are, of course, policies about which the two sides strongly disagree, but that does not mean that the two sides should not work together on policies that they both see as reasonable.

One final point about policies. There may be conflicts between different policies at the state and/or federal level that would have to be dealt with by changes in legislation. For example, removing firearms from those who are at high risk of using them for suicide may run into conflict with the universal background check law (National Instant Criminal Background Check System [NICS]). There may be issues also regarding the length of the temporary removal of the firearms and whether the removal was voluntary or involuntary. Sung (2017) discussed how the state of Washington passed special legislation to resolve some of these issues.

## Conclusions from the Reviews in the Present Book

Having complained about the fact that some researchers do not state their personal opinions about gun control so that the reader of their research can take that into account when assessing their research, I need to state my biases. I grew up in England where gun ownership is rare, where the police require special authorization to take a weapon to a potential crime scene, and where, when I was young, domestic gas was the most common method for suicide. I am in favor of strict gun control.

However, I have been in the United States since 1964, and I know that strict gun control will not occur in the near future, if ever. Therefore, I am in favor of any steps that can be taken in that direction, steps such as requiring safe storage of firearms and working with firearm organizations.

However, as a scientist, I always endeavor to state the results of my research and my reviews of others' research honestly.

The results of the research reviewed in Chapters 1 and 2, as well as the experience of Canada and Australia in Chapters 4 and 5, indicate clearly that firearm availability is associated with firearm suicide. It may be that some of the research fails to support this conclusion, but first, the majority of the studies do support that conclusion and, second, no study finds the reverse association. In other topics in psychological research and social science research, some studies may find positive associations between the variables while others find negative associations. None of the studies reviewed in Chapters 1 and 2 found that, the more firearms, the fewer suicides.

## Substitution of Methods for Suicide

One of the major questions is whether people would switch methods for suicide if firearms were made less available. The fact that some individuals would switch methods is often used as an argument against restricting access to firearms. Several issues are relevant here.

First, it is important to note that this argument is not made against other methods for suicide and has not prevented restricting access to those methods. Bridges from which suicides have jumped to their death have been fenced in, such as the Bloor Street Viaduct in Toronto (Canada). Pills that suicides use for suicidal acts have been dispensed in smaller amounts and encased in plastic blister packs (as in the case of paracetamol [Tylenol] in the United Kingdom). Psychiatric hospitals prevent access to the roofs of their buildings and egress from windows.

Second, there is almost no research on the extent to which people would switch methods for suicide in their preferred method were unavailable. One reason for this is the restriction placed on government funding for research on the use of firearms for suicide, homicide and accidental deaths by the American government. As Lester (2009) has pointed out, in order to explore the possibility of switching methods for suicide more thoroughly, it is important that research be conducted on individuals. How many people do switch methods as they make a series of non-fatal attempts at suicide? What are the most common switches in method, that is, if domestic gas or car exhaust is not available, do those whose who switch have a preferred alternative method? What distinguishes those who switch methods from those who do not? This research has not yet been carried out on potential suicides, although I have carried some research on this issue with samples of undergraduates (see Chapter 1).

Lester, et al. (1989) studied 25 psychiatric inpatients who had made multiple attempts at suicide. Of these 17 (68%) used the same method for suicide, while eight switched method. Those who were switched methods were less often diagnosed as schizophrenic. In a case known to the author, a young woman made multiple attempts at suicide using overdoses of medications but was saved each time. (Social services and family members checked on her daily at her apartment.) She feared to use hanging, a faster and more lethal method. Eventually she was placed on suicide watch in a psychiatric hospital after yet another attempt using an overdose. After one week, she was taken off the suicide watch, whereupon she died by hanging in the hospital. This woman switched from a less lethal method to a more lethal method. If we can increase the chances that people who switch would have to switch from a more lethal method to a less lethal method, then lives may be saved.

The answers to these questions about switching methods for suicide are important when we consider whether restricting access to a lethal method for suicide has an impact on the overall suicide rate (using all methods combined). The research on the detoxification of domestic gas provided an interesting answer to this question. When domestic gas was a very popular method for suicide in a country, the detoxification of domestic gas was accompanied by a reduction in the overall suicide rate. When domestic gas was an uncommon method for suicide in a country, the detoxification of domestic gas had no impact on the overall suicide rate (Lester, 1995).

## FINAL COMMENTS

If restricting access to a lethal method for suicide has no impact on the overall suicide rate, is it worth restricting access to that method? I have always found this question odd because it is never asked in other areas of public health. Government agencies concerned with occupational health and safety remove all hazards from the workplace regardless of whether they save a few lives or many. A medication can be withdrawn if only a few people die from the side-effects regardless of how many people are saved from illness or death for which the medication was designed. In these areas, saving one life is considered to be important. In suicide, saving one life is rarely considered to be as important.

This point is illustrated in a different way by the objection to fencing in bridges from which suicides jump to their death because of esthetic reasons! I put an exclamation point at the end of that sentence because it is amazing to me that those who object on esthetic grounds put so little value on saving lives. Some critics of situational suicide prevention often bring up the possibility that people will switch methods for suicide as an argument for not fencing in the bridge (or restricting other methods for suicide). In the United States, the requirement that backyard swimming pools be fenced in to prevent accidental drownings is not affected by the possibility that people may drown themselves accidentally in lakes, rivers and the oceans. Making the environment safe is a worthy goal even if it cannot be made absolutely safe.

It is noteworthy that the major movements to restrict access to lethal methods for suicide have typically been made on cost or environmental grounds. The use of emission controls on cars was motivated by efforts to reduce pollution. The change from toxic coal gas to less toxic natural gas for domestic use was prompted by cost and pollution considerations. Preventing suicide was not a primary consideration. In contrast, efforts to reduce the widespread availability of pesticides has been motivated by efforts to prevent their use for suicide and accidental deaths. It is possible that restricting access to firearms may occur in the United States in response to murders (and especially mass murders) rather than suicides, and perhaps those restrictions may save some lives from suicide.

## References

Haddon, W. (1973) Energy damage and the 10 countermeasure strategies. *Journal of Trauma*, *13*, 321-331.

Hoyt, T. & Duffy, V. (2015). Implementing firearms restriction for preventing U.S. Army suicide. *Military Psychology*, *27*, 384-390.

Lester, D. (1995). Effects of the detoxification of domestic gas on suicide rates in six nations. *Psychological Reports*, *77*, 294.

Lester, D. (2009). *Preventing suicide: Closing the Exits revisited.* Hauppauge, NY: Nova Science Publishers, Inc.

Lester, D., Fong, C. A. & D'Angelo, A. A. (1989). Chronic suicide attempters who switch methods and those who do not. *Perceptual & Motor Skills*, *69*, 1390.

Lubin, G., Werbeloff, N., Halperin, D., Shmushkevitch, M., Weiser, M. & Knobler, H. Y. (2010). Decrease in suicide rates after a change of policy reducing access to firearms in adolescents. *Suicide & Life-Threatening Behavior*, *40*, 421-424.

Morral, A. R., Schell, T. L. & Tankard, M. (2018). *The magnitude and sources of disagreement among gun policy experts*. Santa Monica, CA: Rand Corporation.

Rand Corporation. (2018). *The science of gun policy*. Santa Monica, CA: Rand Corporation.

Reisch, T., Steffen, T., Habenstein, A. & Tschacher, W. (2013). Change in suicide rates in Switzerland before and after firearm restriction resulting from the 2003 "Army XXI" reform. *American Journal of Psychiatry*, *170*, 977-984.

Runyan, C. W., Brown, T. L. & Brooks-Russell, A. (2015). Preventing the invisible plague of firearm suicide. *American Journal of Orthopsychiatry*, *85*, 321-324.

Sung, J. C. (2017). Firearms policy and suicide prevention. *American Journal of Psychiatry*, *174*, 1223.

# EDITOR CONTACT INFORMATION

***David Lester, PhD***
Professor Emeritus
Stockton University,
Galloway, New Jersey, US
Email: lesterd@stockton.edu

# List of Contributors

**John F. Gunn III, MA**
Department of Family Science and Human Development
Montclair State University, New Jersey, US
Email: gunnj3@montclair.edu.

**Karolina Krysinska, PhD**
Center for Mental Health, Melbourne School of Population & Global Health,
University of Melbourne, Victoria, Australia;
Center for Primary Health Care & Equity,
University of New South Wales, Sydney, Australia
Email: k.krysinska@unsw.edu.au

**Karin Lavoie, MLS**
Centre for Suicide Prevention, Calgary, Alberta, Canada
Email: karin@suicideinfo.ca

**Antoon A. Leenaars, PhD, CPsych, CPQ**
Private Practice, Windsor, Ontario, Canada
Email: draalee@sympatico.ca

**Robert Olson, MLS**
Centre for Suicide Prevention, Calgary, Alberta, Canada
Email: robert@suicideinfo.ca

# INDEX

## A



## B



## C



## D



## E



## F

## R



## S



## U



## V



## W



## Y

## Understanding Impulsive Behavior: Assessment, Influences and Gender Differences

**Editor:** Christian Braddon

**Series:** Psychology of Emotions, Motivations and Actions

**Book Description:** In this compilation, the authors begin by describing the main impulsive behavior assessment instruments in animals and humans.


**Softcover ISBN:** 978-1-53613-815-3
**Retail Price:** $95


## Studies in the Evolutionary Psychology of Feeling

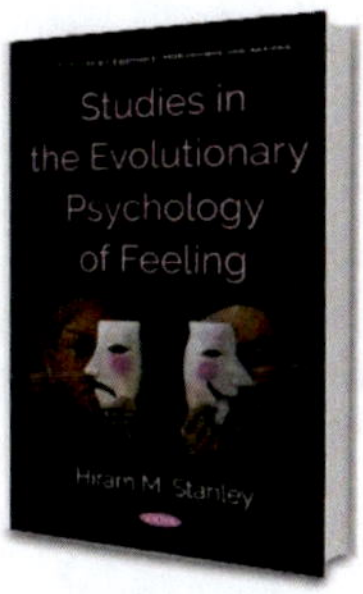


**Editor:** Hiram M. Stanley

**Series:** Psychology of Emotions, Motivations and Actions

**Book Description:** This work, originally published in 1895, does not profess to be a treatise on the subject of feeling, but merely a series of studies, and rather tentative ones at that.


**Hardcover ISBN:** 978-1-53614-483-3
**Retail Price:** $230